Sweet & Simple
handmade

Melissa Wastney

25 Projects to Sew, Stitch, Knit & Upcycle for Children

stashBOOKS.
an imprint of C&T Publishing

Text and Style Photography copyright © 2013 by Melissa Wastney

Subject Photography copyright © 2013 by C&T Publishing, Inc.

Illustrations copyright © 2013 by C&T Publishing, Inc.

Publisher: Amy Marson

Creative Director: Gailen Runge

Art Director/Cover Designer: Kristy Zacharias

Editors: Cynthia Bix and Jill Mordick

Technical Editors: Ann Haley and Amanda Siegfried

Book Designer: April Mostek

Page Layout Artist: Kerry Graham

Production Coordinator: Zinnia Heinzmann

Production Editor: Joanna Burgarino

Illustrator: Valyrie Friedman

Photography by Christina Carty-Francis and Diane Pedersen of C&T Publishing, Inc.,
unless otherwise noted

Published by Stash Books, an imprint of C&T Publishing, Inc., P.O. Box 1456,
Lafayette, CA 94549

Library of Congress Cataloging-in-Publication Data

Wastney, Melissa, 1980-

 Sweet & simple handmade : 25 projects to sew, stitch, knit & upcycle for children / Melissa
Wastney.

   pages cm

 ISBN 978-1-60705-665-2

1. Sewing. 2. Knitting--Patterns. 3. Clothing and dress--Remaking. I. Title. II. Title:
Sweet and simple handmade.

 TT715.W37 2013

 646'.1--dc23

              2012035173

Printed in China

10 9 8 7 6 5 4 3 2 1

Dedication

I dedicate this book to my family, with love.

Acknowledgments

I had such fun making this book! But I couldn't have done it without many of the great people around me. Thanks to Francesca, Charlotte, Michal, and Jenny, who, in different ways, planted the seed of writing this book in my mind. Thanks to Rachelle and Susie for their encouragement and support. Also to Kirsty, Karina, Jess, Adele, and Karuna for their love and friendship. Then to Sarah Laing, Helen Lehndorf, and Emma McCleary for that encouraging coffee date in an Auckland café last year.

Thank you to the team at Stash Books—especially Susanne, Diane, Cynthia, and Amy.

The biggest thank-yous must go to my patient family—Tom, Arlo, and Keira—who endured many grumpy times, fittings, and photo sessions with grace. Thanks too to my parents, Ian and Sally, for believing in and encouraging me; Clare and Dave and whanau for their love and support; Nick and Clare for friendship and a tripod; and Tamsin, Tristan, Alexander, and Sarah, my sweet siblings.

Thank you to my dear blog readers, followers, and customers from all over the world.

And, of course, to my beautiful models—thank you for letting me work with you! Thank you to Millie, Guy, Noa, Eve, Richie, Arlo, Xavier, Bernadette, and Keira; my nephew, Leo; and, of course, my gorgeous nieces, Esmae, Phoebe, Fern, Noa, and Eve, who have provided me with so much inspiration over the past ten years.

Contents

Introduction   6

Creative Upcycling ◆ Before You Start
Involving Children ◆ Size Chart

Introduction ----------------------------------

Kia ora! as we say in New Zealand.

Welcome to my book of patterns and designs for the children in your life. I imagine that you are either a parent or grandparent of a young child, or that maybe you have small friends or family members for whom you wish to make something.

In writing this book, my main aim was to collect together designs that might be truly useful for the home sewer with small people (children under about ten years old) around. I wanted to make an appealing book to be turned to often for inspiration and basic patterns. Most of my designs are not particularly fancy; they owe their specialness to the fabrics and embellishments used. I hope that my interpretations of these designs will inspire you to go and be creative with them.

I have always been interested in creativity and crafts, but it wasn't until I was pregnant with my son, Arlo, in 2002 that I rekindled my own childhood obsession with making things and looking for inspiration all around me. I was keen to stay at home for the years that my two children were preschoolers; it seemed like a good decision for our family. We made do with our slim income by making lots of things ourselves, from bedding and toys to clothes and gardens. It's easy to glorify those times. The truth is that they were challenging, but they were made easier by my decision to be at home every day of the week. Now our situation has eased a bit, but I still love to make things. I find that I am constantly inspired by the natural world, as well as by traditional handwork, vintage ceramics, and fabric. My friends and family—many of whom are artists, designers, writers, and musicians—are also a source of inspiration.

Creative Upcycling

Buying secondhand is still a priority for our family, as I'm sure it is for a growing number of people—if my recent trips to garage sales and secondhand markets are any indication. Old things that still work (I'm thinking here of equipment like irons and sewing machines) tend to do so for longer than new ones, even if they don't come with a twelve-month warranty. They just seem to be built better. Buying secondhand is more affordable, too, and the profits often benefit local charities and churches. But I think the biggest benefit of buying secondhand goods is the recycling aspect. Knowing that you are using something already in existence, rather than creating more waste and packaging, is a very good feeling.

I write here about "thinking secondhand" because there are many opportunities for us to do so in our creative work. If you keep an open mind, you can find good fabric everywhere, even without spending much money. Your first stop should of course be your local fabric and yarn store, if you have one. This is an invaluable resource for interesting supplies and good craft advice.

As for secondhand items, you can find them in thrift stores, in antique shops, on online auction sites such as eBay and Trade Me (New Zealand's version of eBay), and at garage sales. Many of the fabrics used in this book were found secondhand. Discarded curtains, linens, and tablecloths can make great bags, while old sheets and duvet covers can be used for linings and to make trial versions of patterns.

If you are seriously interested in upcycling fabrics for sewing, put the word out to your family and friends that you would be happy to reuse any textiles they are discarding. Your next biggest problem might be finding somewhere to store them all!

Before You Start

There are no firm "rules" you must follow when creating upcycled children's items, but here are a few notes and guidelines.

+ All the seam allowances in the patterns are ¼", unless otherwise indicated.

+ Many of the tissue paper patterns are handily located in this book and are graded for a range of sizes. You can either cut the patterns out and keep them in a separate envelope for later use or trace the patterns onto newsprint paper as you need them. If you do cut them out from the sheet entirely, remember to cut the largest size given and fold over the extra paper. You can also use a warm iron on your paper patterns to get them in shape before pinning them to your fabric.

+ When directed to cut two of any pattern, place the pattern on two layers of fabric with right sides together, unless otherwise instructed.

+ Remember to wash, dry, and press your fabrics before use, to prevent shrinkage or color bleeding.

+ Good music in the background and a cup of tea on the table will make your work more enjoyable. Believe me.

+ The patterns in this book are a collection of things that I have designed and made countless times over the past ten years. They've been made as gifts, upon request from my children and their friends, and for my own online shop (see page 144) and other stores around the world. Every item has been made with a lot of thought and love, and, I hope, a little of my own childhood dreaming is stitched in too.

I hope you enjoy making these projects as much as I do.

Involving Children

The projects in this book are designed with the home crafter in mind. I'm imagining someone who moonlights as a creative type in the evenings but during the day cares for small children— someone like a parent, grandparent, aunt or uncle, godparent, nanny, or friend.

If you like making things for children, you probably like working on projects with them, too. While it can be tricky to find the patience and energy to tackle a complicated project such as knitting or embroidery with children (at least it is for me), there are other ways in which they can be involved in your "making."

If your children show an interest, hand over your craft books and ask for their feedback and input. If there's a project they are drawn to, you can encourage them to choose a suitable fabric from your stash to make it, or you can go shopping together for the materials. Remember to keep it simple and low-key, and when you are fabric shopping, quick trips are preferable. My children really enjoy wandering through a big fabric store, touching all the different textures, and sometimes hiding among the bolts (our local shop has understanding and tolerant staff members!).

It can be fun to hand your children a stack of paper and pens and encourage them to design their dream T-shirt, ideal pair of summer pants, or whatever. Take into account their favorite colors and motifs and work those into the finished garment.

Be careful not to force any unwilling children into the crafty process. We want them to come to it when they are motivated and ready. If your child does seem interested, he or she can help with cutting and tracing patterns, pinning the paper patterns to the fabric, and cutting around them. Children can do any or all of these steps if you're willing to let them. There's no better way to learn than by doing.

The next step is to teach your child to use a sewing machine, which he or she can do from quite a young age—if given a lesson on the potential dangers of sewing over a finger! It can take a while to learn to control the speed of the machine pedal; this learning is best done on scrap fabric, of course. When I was about eleven years old, my parents bought me an old but sturdy Bernina sewing machine to practice on, and it was most liberating and educational!

Some of the projects in this book would make wonderful adult-child collaborations. The pom-pom hat and matching scarf (pages 130–137) provide the perfect opportunity to get your kids making pom-poms, an activity that gave me many hours of happiness as a little one.

Finally, even if the children in your household show very little interest in making things themselves, by working on projects when they are nearby, you are showing them that it is fun and rewarding to do creative work and make things ourselves. And, of course, that is just one of the benefits of "making" at home. We can also show our children how to better care for the environment around them, show love and affection for friends and family, and sidestep the damaging consumer culture that permeates our society.

I hope you enjoy making these projects for and with the children in your life. Above all, these projects are supposed to be fun!

Size Chart Note: *Sizes are approximate only and based on average child sizes.*

Follow the measurements listed below to choose the correct pattern size.

Age	US size	Height	Weight (approximately)	Chest measurement (approximately)	Waist measurement (approximately)
Babies 6–12 months	Up to 24 months	Up to 34″	16–28 pounds	19″–21″	17″–20″
Toddlers 1–4 years	2T–4T/4	35″–43″	24–41 pounds	21″–23″	19″–21″
Children 5–10 years	5–6X	46″–50″	42–54 pounds	24″–26″	22″–26″

16

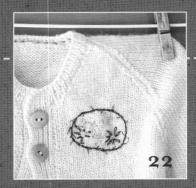

22

26

32

36

40

46

For Babies

ages 0—12 months

Reversible Baby Shoes --------------

Sizes: 0–6 months to fit a baby foot up to 4˝ long

6–12 months to fit a baby foot up to 4½˝ long

I first designed this pattern in 2005

when my daughter, Keira, was born. I made a pair for her with yellow poppies on the toes. Then I made pairs for my nieces and friends' kids. Since then I've made a lot of these little shoes. I hope you'll enjoy making a pair for your little one. Some of the interior seams can be a little tricky. I suggest having a trial run first—after all, each pair uses very little fabric.

Due to their fabric soles, these slippers are designed for pre-walkers. You could sew small scraps of suede for the outer soles, though, if you like. Make them in newborn size, 0–6 months, or for older babies, 6–12 months.

I like to use the best parts of old embroidered linens, thereby giving them a new lease on life and passing them on to another generation. Bold cotton prints work well, too.

You will need

¼ yard of cotton or linen fabric for the outer shoe

¼ yard of fine cotton or linen fabric for the lining

7″ × 8″ piece of cotton corduroy (nonstretch) for the outer sole

7″ × 8″ piece of stretch-cotton fabric for the sole lining*

10″ length of narrow elastic (I used ¼″-wide white braided elastic.)

* You could recycle an old T-shirt for this.

Cutting

Trace the pattern pieces (on tissue paper pattern sheet) for the shoe upper, sole, and heel in your desired size.

Outer shoe fabric

Cut 2 heel pieces and 2 upper pieces.

Lining fabric

Cut 2 heel pieces and 2 upper pieces.

Stretch cotton

Cut 2 sole pieces.

Corduroy

Cut 2 sole pieces.

Elastic

Cut 2 lengths 4½″ for size 0–6 months or 2 lengths 4¾″ for size 6–12 months.

Let's make them

1. Make the heel by placing 1 heel lining piece and 1 heel outer piece right sides together. Sew them together along 1 long edge. Turn right side out and press. Sew ½" from the pressed seam to create a channel for threading the elastic.

2. Attach a small safety pin to the end of an elastic piece. Carefully thread this through the channel until the end of the elastic is aligned with the raw edge of the heel piece. Secure the end in place by sewing back and forth close to the fabric edge. Continue drawing the elastic through the channel until the safety pin comes out the other end. Stitch down this end of the elastic.

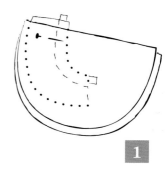

3. Repeat Steps 1 and 2 with the second shoe.

4. To sew the shoe uppers to the elasticized heel, start by placing 1 upper piece in the lining fabric and 1 upper piece in the outer fabric, right sides together. Slip 1 finished heel piece between the uppers, so that the heel outer fabric is facing the upper outer fabric (Figure 1). The heel's side edge should extend about ¾" beyond the straight edge of the uppers. Pin in place.

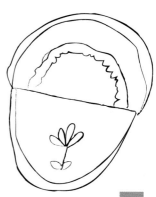

5. Now stretch the upper edge around the other end of the heel piece and pin it in place on the other side (Figure 2).

6. Stitch carefully along the straight edge of the upper, securing all the layers in the seam. Turn the uppers right side out and press (Figure 3).

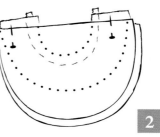

7. Repeat Steps 4–6 with the second shoe pieces.

8. Sew the soles to the prepared heel/upper arrangement. I find this easiest to do on my lap. Place a stretch-cotton sole right side up on your thigh, with the toe pointing toward your knee. Place the assembled heel/upper on top of this piece, right side up, matching the toe edges and holding them in place with your fingers. Now place a corduroy sole on top of the shoe upper, right side down and, again, matching the toe curve. Hold all the layers together at the toe edge and sew around this curve, securing all the layers in the seam. Sew down the right side of the slipper. You'll have to remove it from the sewing machine and align the layers a little so you can catch them in your next seam. Repeat down the left side of the slipper. Leave an opening at the heel.

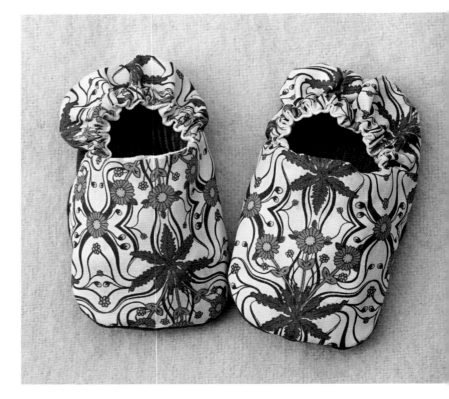

9. Now turn the slipper right side out (the stretch cotton makes this easier) and check the seams to ensure that there are no openings. If there are, you might need to unpick the seams and try again. Keep in mind that this step requires a little patience and practice. Turn the slipper inside out again and give it another try. When you're happy with your sewing, turn the slipper inside out again and sew around the same seam a couple more times to ensure that it's secure while leaving an opening at the heel. Trim around the seam closely and carefully, following the curve.

10. Repeat Steps 8 and 9 with the second slipper.

11. Turn both slippers right side out. Now hand sew the openings you left for turning both slippers. Use strong cotton thread and a sharp needle. Sew the outer layers together first with

small, neat stitches. You will be turning the corduroy edge under as you go and slightly gathering the heel piece to fit. Then bring the thread to the lining side and stitch to close the lining opening. Secure the thread before finishing.

For gift giving, you could add a little tag explaining that the slippers are to be hand washed and place some tissue paper inside to make sure they retain their shape.

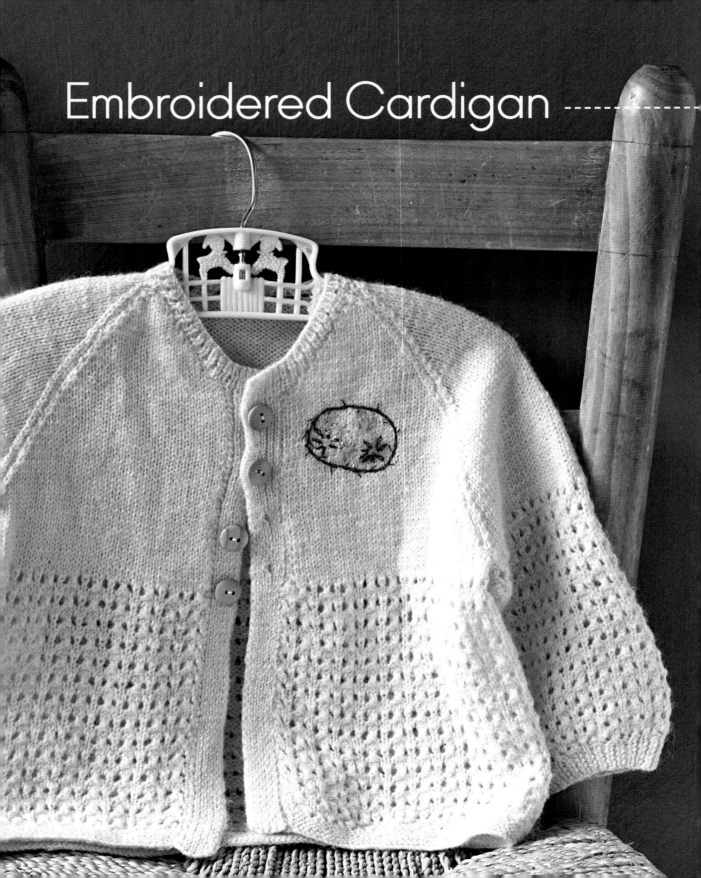

Embroidered Cardigan -------------

I'm always looking for ways to reuse old things, and this project makes a sweet gift for a new baby, while being eco-friendly too. Hunt in your local secondhand shops or markets for baby knitwear in classic shapes and colors. Look for pure wool garments; they wear and wash better. It's best to use pieces that are in good condition, but a few small holes can always be carefully mended. And, of course, this technique could be used on any vintage knitwear: sweaters, little suits, or bonnets.

I found the little cardigan pictured at my local Save the Children shop and replaced the buttons to match my hand embroidery.

You will need

Knitted wool cardigan or sweater in a plain color

Embroidery floss in various colors

Let's make it

1. Carefully hand wash the garment and dry it flat on a towel. Check for any marks or holes and mend as necessary.

2. Work your embroidery, using the stitches and designs shown in Embroidery Ideas (page 24) as a guide if you like.

3. Replace the buttons if desired.

Adding a bit of embroidery can give any garment an extra-special touch. Here are some basic stitches that I like to use, as well as some diagrams for motifs that I embroider often.

Stitches

Satin Stitch

Couching

Cross Stitch

Chain Stitch

Backstitch

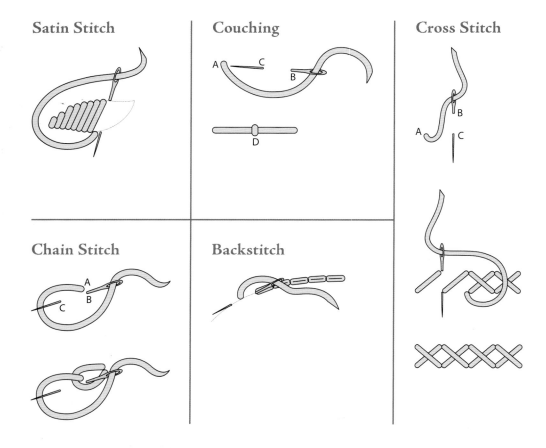

Embroidery design ideas

Feather

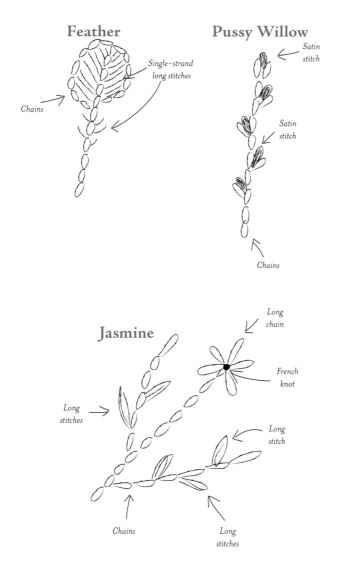

Single-strand
long stitches

Chains

Pussy Willow

Satin
stitch

Satin
stitch

Chains

Daisy

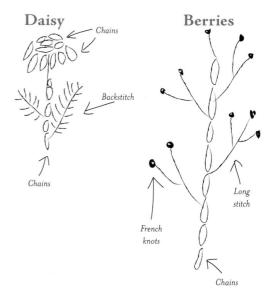

Chains

Backstitch

Chains

Berries

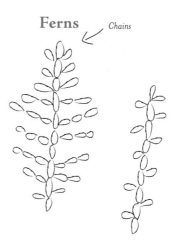

Long
stitch

French
knots

Chains

Jasmine

Long
chain

French
knot

Long
stitch

Long
stitches

Chains

Long
stitches

Ferns

Chains

Starry Sky Baby Quilt

Finished quilt: 36½˝ × 60½˝
Finished Sawtooth Star block: 12˝ × 12˝

Anyone who has had a long pregnancy

knows how slowly those last weeks can go by (especially if it's a first baby). Prepare for the arrival of your little one by making one of these simple little crib quilts, while enjoying the starry, peaceful evenings on your own before everything changes.

This quilt is made up of seven Sawtooth Star blocks interspersed with eight cream cotton blocks to help the pieced blocks really stand out and to keep the whole project nice and simple. I love to recycle fabrics, and in the original spirit of quiltmaking, I decided to use some work shirts belonging to my partner, Tom, to make the stars on this baby quilt. I chose only those that he was discarding (because they were well-worn or stained with pen ink) and that were 100% cotton in composition. The finished quilt will smell slightly of a father, which is always nice, and the recycled cotton is extra soft and cozy. I like the simple blue and red color scheme that, combined with the star theme, makes this quilt perfect for either a small girl or boy. Of course, you could recycle any clothing (meaningful or not), such as dresses or skirts, other children's clothes, or thrift shop finds.

You will need

2½ yards of cotton cream fabric

3 or 4 cotton shirts or other fabric
for the Sawtooth Star blocks*

41″ × 65″ piece of cotton fabric for the backing

41″ × 65″ piece of wool or cotton quilt batting

6 yards of double-fold bias tape or quilt binding

Approximately 50 safety pins

** Alternately, 7 fat quarters or 1¼ yards
fabric may be used for the stars.*

Cutting

Cream fabric

Cut 28 squares 3½″ × 3½″ for
the Sawtooth Star blocks.

Cut 28 rectangles 3½″ × 6½″
for the Sawtooth Star blocks.

Cut 8 squares 12½″ × 12½″
for the setting squares.

Shirt or other fabric

Cut 7 squares 6½″ × 6½″ for the
Sawtooth Star block centers.

Cut 56 squares 3½″ × 3½″ for
the Sawtooth Star block points.

TIP
Remember:

⁃ Wash and press all your fabrics before you start.

⁃ Sew each seam with a ¼″ seam allowance.

⁃ Neatly press each seam open after sewing.

Let's make the stars

1. Iron each of the 3½″ × 3½″ shirt squares in half diagonally to create a creased line down the middle. Open the squares and pin to an end of a 3½″ × 6½″ cream rectangle with right sides together, so that the diagonal creased line is running from the bottom left-hand corner to the middle of the top of the cream rectangle (Figure 1).

2. Sew down the diagonal fold on the square (Figure 2). Press again. Trim away the excess fabric using your rotary cutter, as shown.

3. Open the triangle and press (Figure 3).

4. Repeat Steps 1–3 using another of the 3½″ × 3½″ squares on the other end of the cream rectangle to create a Flying Geese unit (Figure 4). Make 4 Flying Geese units.

5. Arrange the Sawtooth Star block as shown (Figure 5). Sew the pieces in 3 rows and then sew the rows together. Press the finished block.

6. Repeats Steps 1–5 to complete a total of 7 Sawtooth Star blocks.

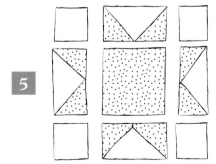

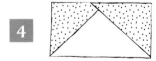

Let's make the quilt

1. Arrange the 12½″ × 12½″ squares of cream cotton and the star blocks as shown (Figure 6) and sew into rows. Press the seams open. Sew the block rows together. Press the finished quilt top.

2. Make the quilt backing by either cutting a single piece of fabric or sewing together pieces of leftover fabric to measure at least 2″ larger than the quilt top on all sides (approximately 41″ × 65″).

3. Cut the quilt batting so that it is the same size as the quilt back from Step 2. Make a sandwich by laying the quilt backing on the floor, wrong side up, then the batting on top of it, and then the quilt top, right side up. Position the layers so that the quilt top is centered on the batting and backing.

6   Assembly diagram

4. Smooth the 3 layers and then pin through all the layers with safety pins. I try to pin all around the quilt edge and then place a pin in each square. Be careful not to pin over any of the block seams.

5. Take the pinned quilt to your sewing machine and, using matching thread, carefully sew in-the-ditch of each block and each star.

6. Remove all the safety pins except those around the edge. Keep the batting untrimmed for now. Apply bias tape or binding all around the edge (if you need help with this, there are many great tutorials on YouTube or quilting websites).

7. Carefully trim the excess batting and backing close to the bias tape. Remove any remaining pins. Hand stitch the binding to the back of the quilt. The quilt can look extra inviting after a machine wash and tumble dry. You're done. Congratulations!

Soft and Stretchy Pants

Sizes (by baby's height):
0–6 months, 29˝
6–12 months, 34˝

These are comfortable and soft pants

that make a useful staple in a baby's wardrobe. If you use pure cotton knit fabric, they will become softer with each wash. This pattern is especially designed to fit over a cloth-diapered bottom but will fit for a few years after that, as shorter pants. In fact, my daughter (aged six and petite) still wears her baby pants under dresses! You can customize these simple pants in any way you choose by adding embroidery, appliqué, or even a rather unnecessary but sweet little pocket.

You will need

---

1 yard of stretch-cotton fabric (¾ yard will be enough for the smallest size.)

24″ length of 2″-wide flat elastic

Cutting

Trace the pattern piece (on tissue paper pattern sheet) in the desired size.

Cut 2 pants pieces.

Cut an elastic length to fit around your baby's waist plus a ½″ overlap; otherwise use this general guide: newborn size, 17″; 6 months, 19″; 1 year, 20″.

TIPS

· When sewing with stretch fabric, look for the firmer variety that is 100% cotton. This is easier to sew and wears better, too.

· Stretch cotton is much easier to sew with a longer stitch setting on your machine. Try not to pull and stretch the fabric as you sew.

· Make sure you use a new and very sharp needle on your machine for best results. You can also purchase a special jersey needle for this type of sewing.

· I like to hand stitch a small loop made from cotton tape to the back waistband of the pants, to help with dressing.

Let's make them

1. With right sides together, sew the 2 pants pieces together along the front center using a ¼″ seam allowance. Align the pieces along the back center seam with right sides together and sew the back center seam. Finish the seams by serging or zigzagging the raw edges.

2. Align the inner leg edges and pin. Stitch the inner leg seam as a continuous seam (Figure 1). Resew this seam again to reinforce the stitching. Turn the pants right side out.

3. Using a warm iron, press under ¼″ along the top of the pants. The back edge of the pants is cut higher than the front edge. Fold this seam down again to make a 2¼″ casing (just a little wider than the 2″-wide elastic). Press in place, and pin if necessary. Sew the casing in place along the lower edge, leaving a 2″ opening at the center back for inserting the elastic. Topstitch close to the top of the casing too, if you wish.

4. Cut the length of elastic to size. Attach a safety pin to an end and thread it through the opening in the casing. Be careful to keep it flat and untwisted as you thread it around the top of the pants. Overlap the elastic ends ½″ and stitch together. Stitch the opening in the casing to close.

5. Fold and press a ¼″ hem on each leg. Fold under again ¼″ and pin in place if necessary. Sew around each leg.

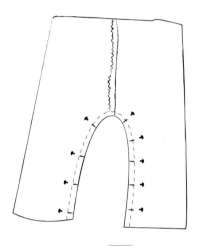

1

Modern Bonnet

Sizes: 0–6 months, head circumference approximately 14″–15″

6–12 months, head circumference approximately 16″–17″

I've always loved
old-fashioned baby clothes,
and the bonnet used to be a layette staple.
These slightly modernized hats are so sweet
and can be customized by using different
fabrics and embellishments. A cotton version
makes a great sun hat, while a bonnet made
from wool and lined in soft flannel will keep
a little one's ears warm on an outing to a
windy beach.

You will need

½ yard of sturdy cotton, corduroy, or wool fabric for the bonnet outer

½ yard of soft cotton, lawn, or flannel fabric for the lining

1 yard of ribbon or cotton tape

Cutting

Trace the pattern pieces (on tissue paper pattern sheet) for the bonnet back and bonnet side.

Outer fabric

Cut 1 each of the back and side pieces in the desired size.

Lining fabric

Cut 1 each of the back and side pieces.

Let's make it

1. Using the longest stitch setting on your sewing machine, baste along the long curved edge of the outer bonnet side piece, between the notches. Gather these stitches until the gathered edge is the same length as the curved edge of the outer bonnet back piece. Pin the side to the back with right sides together. Stitch using a regular stitch length. Remove the basting stitches and press. Repeat with the side and back lining pieces. Embellish the exterior of the bonnet, if desired (see Variations, page 39).

2. Cut the ribbon or cotton tape in half. Snip small triangles at one end of each piece to stop fraying. Pin the other ends to the bonnet exterior, as shown (Figure 1).

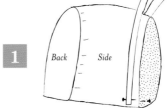

1   Back   Side

3. Ensure that the bonnet lining is turned inside out and the bonnet exterior is right side out. Place the bonnet exterior inside the bonnet lining so the right sides are facing and the bonnet ties are encased inside the layers. Pin around all the edges, leaving an opening of about 3″ at the back center. Sew all around this seam, leaving the opening unsewn.

4. Clip the seam close to the stitching and trim the corners. Turn the bonnet right side out through the opening. Press. Hand stitch the opening closed. Topstitch around the edge, if desired.

Variations

You can add embroidery to the side of the bonnet, as I have on my niece's hat. It can be fun to mimic the print on the bonnet lining.

You could also add an appliquéd patch of the lining fabric to the side of the bonnet. It's best to make any embellishments like this before sewing the bonnet lining and exterior together.

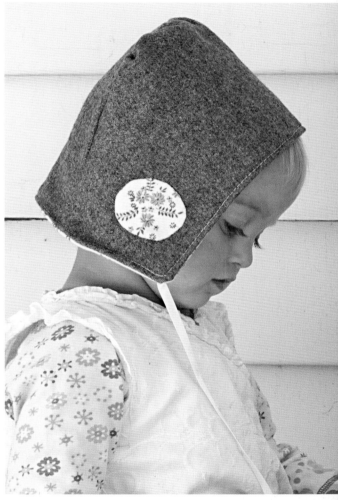

Linen Teddy

Finished toy:

13½˝ from top of head to toe

A special soft toy (or "lovey," as they
are sometimes known here in the Antipodes)
is a must for a new baby. A beautiful handmade
animal makes a great gift—one that might
accompany the child as he or she grows up and
may eventually become a treasured heirloom.
This is my pattern for a simple teddy with a
friendly face, made from classic natural linen.

You will need

½ yard of natural linen
fabric in any shade*

4″ × 6″ scrap of printed cotton
fabric for the ear linings

Cotton, wool, or polyester stuffing

1-yard length of satin or velvet ribbon

Embroidery thread and a small hoop

** If you are having trouble finding linen in your
town, try looking in secondhand shops for linen
shirts, dresses, or pants with a minimum of seams.
Carefully dissected, linen garments can provide
enough high-quality linen for handmade toys.*

Cutting

Trace the pattern pieces (on tissue
paper pattern sheet) for the bear's
body, arms, legs, and ears.

Linen fabric
Cut 2 body pieces, 2 ear pieces,
4 arm pieces, and 4 leg pieces.

Printed cotton fabric
Cut 2 ear pieces.

Let's make it

1. With right sides together, sew around 2 arm pieces using a ¼"
seam allowance. Leave the top end open for turning. For extra
strength, I like to sew these seams twice and iron the stitches before
turning. Repeat with the remaining arm and leg pieces to make a total
of 2 arms and 2 legs.

2. Cut close to the stitching around the curves and, using the eraser
end of a pencil, turn the legs and arms right side out. Lightly stuff the
arms and legs with stuffing. Set aside.

3. Following the guidelines on the body paper pattern, make 2 small
darts at the top of the head on both pieces. Press, pin, and stitch the
darts. Trim the excess and press flat.

4. Using the pattern sheet as a guide, trace the bear face markings
onto one of the body pieces with a soft pencil. Place the piece inside
the embroidery hoop and work the facial features in a dark brown
thread over the pencil markings. I like to use a fine thread, with a
small backstitch for the mouth and a satin stitch for the nose and
eyes. When you're happy with the face, remove the fabric from the
hoop, carefully erase any visible pencil marks, and press the wrong
side with a warm iron.

5. Make the ears by sewing together 1 linen ear piece and 1 cotton
ear piece, right sides together, leaving the bottom edge open. Clip
close to the stitching and turn right side out. Press. Pinch the raw
edge together to create a small pleat in the ear. Sew across this raw
edge on your machine to secure the pleat (Figure 1). Repeat with the
remaining ear pieces.

6. Lay the bear front piece on a flat surface, right side up, and place one completed ear cotton-side down, with the raw edge matching the raw edge of the bear body piece. Align the center of the ear with the small dart you sewed earlier and pin in place. Repeat with the second ear (Figure 2). Machine sew the ears in place, close to the edge of the bear body piece.

7. On a flat surface, arrange the bear body front, right side up, and, following the pattern guidelines, lay the stuffed bear arms in place, raw edges matching (Figure 3). Lay the bear body back piece on the front with right sides together, sandwiching the ears and arms inside. Pin the arms in place, and pin all around the bear head, including the ears.

8. Now sew the top half of the body pieces together, beginning just below one arm and finishing just below the other. Turn the bear right side out and check that the arms are even and everything looks okay; then turn it inside out again and restitch for strength. Press the seam with a warm iron.

9. Place one of the stuffed legs inside the bear body so that the raw edge is aligned with the bottom of the bear body. Repeat with the other leg. Pin in place and sew around the lower part of the bear body, leaving an opening on one side (Figure 4). This is a tricky step, but be patient and check that you are catching all the edges together in the seam. Sew the seam at the bottom again to ensure that the legs are well attached.

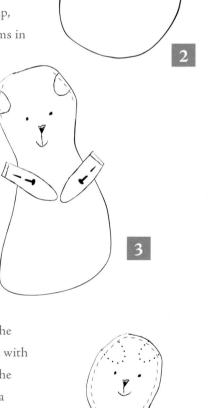

2

3

Opening

4

10. Carefully turn the bear right side out through the opening you left. You will need to do this slowly, pulling out a bear limb at a time. If you are pleased with the limb placement, you can stuff the bear through the opening. Hand stitch the opening closed with small and secure stitches.

11. Tie the ribbon around your teddy's neck.

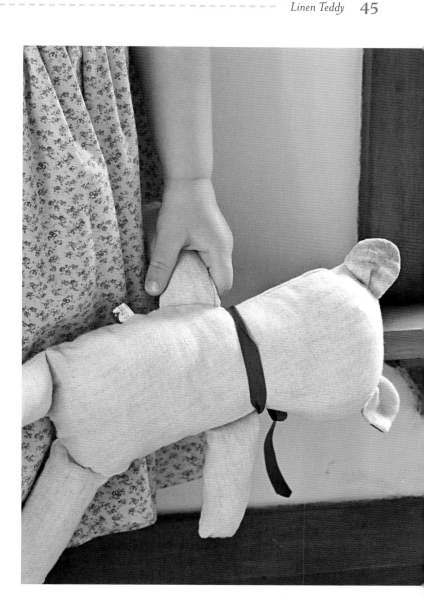

New Mama "Everything" Tote ------

Finished tote:

15˝ across bag top × 14˝ tall

Don't forget a gift for the new mama!

A bag is a lovely way to wrap up a little something for the new baby and her mother, too. This bag pattern has been my old faithful since I had my first baby eight years ago. It is light and easy to carry, looks stylish, and can carry a surprising amount of stuff—all essential factors for a busy mother on the go.

You will need

1 yard of fabric for the bag exterior. I like to use something sturdy for this, but it must be nonstretch. Linen, corduroy, and cotton canvas are all good choices. You could recycle something like a stylish old curtain, if you like.

1 yard of fabric for the bag lining. Cotton calico is my favorite. It's best to use something lightweight and light in color for easy finding of keys, for example.

Cutting

Trace the pattern pieces (on tissue paper pattern sheet) for the bag's top panel, lower panel, and lining.

Outer fabric

Cut 2 top panel pieces and 2 lower panel pieces.

Cut 2 pieces 2½″ × 20″ for the handles.

Lining fabric

Cut 2 bag lining pieces.

Cut 2 pieces 2½″ × 20″ for the handles.

Cut 2 pieces 4″ × 7″ for the pocket.

Let's make it

1. Lay 1 bag exterior lower panel so that the edge with the little corners cut out is at the bottom and the straight edge is at the top. Pin 4 pleats 1″ deep along the top edge, as shown on the pattern (Figure 1). Repeat with the second lower panel.

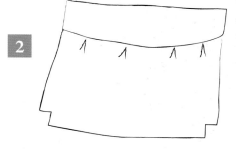

2. Lay 1 bag exterior upper panel right sides together with a bag exterior lower panel. Pin so the top edge of the lower panel fits the slightly curved edge of the upper panel and stitch. Use a warm iron to press the seam toward the upper panel (Figure 2). Topstitch with matching or contrasting thread. Repeat with the other bag exterior panels.

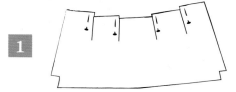

3. With right sides together and taking care to match the panel seams on each side of the bag, stitch the sides and bottom of the completed bag exterior pieces. Leave the top of the bag unstitched. Reinforce the seams on the sides of the bag, where the panels meet. Pinch a notched corner so the notch becomes a straight line. Stitch ¼″ from the straight line. Repeat with the other notched corner. Set the bag exterior aside.

4. Place the 2 pocket pieces right sides together and sew along all the sides with a ¼″ seam allowance, leaving a small opening in the middle of the top seam. Clip the corners and turn right side out. Press flat. Topstitch along the pocket top, closing the opening as you go.

5. Fold 1 lining piece in half to find the middle point. Center the completed pocket piece, using the folded line as a guide. Pin around the sides and bottom. Stitch the pocket to the bag lining (Figure 3).

6. Place the 2 lining pieces right sides together and sew along the sides and bottom, leaving the top open. Pinch out the corners and sew across this seam about 2″ from the point (Figure 4).

7. Place 1 handle piece right sides together with 1 handle lining piece and sew, stitching down the 2 long sides with a ¼″ seam. Press the seams. Turn right side out and press again. Topstitch along both sewn edges of the handle. Repeat with the remaining pieces to make a second handle.

8. Turn the completed bag exterior right side out and lay it on a flat surface with the bag back facing up. Turn the bag lining inside out with the pocket side facing up, and place the bag exterior inside the lining. Align and pin the top edges.

9. Place 1 handle piece inside the bag, between the exterior and lining, so the unfinished edges are just poking out the top. The handle lining side should face the bag lining. Align the unfinished handle edges so they are evenly spaced from the side seams of the bag. Pin in place. Repeat with the other handle on the other side of the bag. Check that the handles are exactly opposite each other (Figure 5).

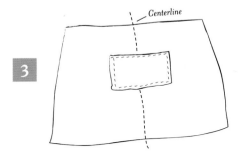

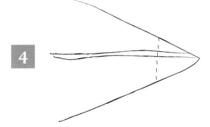

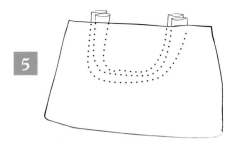

10. Sew around the top seam of the bag layers, making sure you are including both the lining and the exterior, as well as the handles when you come to them. Leave an opening between the back handle edges. Remove the pins and turn the bag right side out through the opening. Push the lining into the outer bag.

11. Press the bag around the top edge and place a pin in the opening to hold the layers together. Topstitch around the entire top edge of the bag, closing the opening as you go.

54

58

62

68

72

76

80

84

90

For Little Ones

ages 1–4

Corduroy Pants to Grow In

Sizes: 2T–4T

These corduroy pants are a favorite in my circle of friends—I have made countless pairs as gifts. Cotton corduroy is a comfortable, sturdy fabric that washes and wears well, and it has nostalgic value for most parents, too. This particular design is great for quickly growing children because it is roomy and the legs can be rolled up and then gradually let down over time. The pants can be customized and made extra-useful with patch pockets from bright and friendly cotton prints.

You will need

1 yard of cotton corduroy fabric, nonstretch

12″ × 14″ piece of contrasting cotton fabric for the pockets and pocket lining

1″-wide elastic, enough to fit snugly around the child's waist, plus overlap (approximately 20″–22″)

Cutting

Trace the pattern pieces (on tissue paper pattern sheet) for the pants back, pants front, and pocket in the selected size (see Note, at right).

Cotton fabric
Cut 4 pocket pieces.

Corduroy fabric
Cut 2 front pieces and 2 back pieces.

NOTE

These pants can easily be lengthened to fit your child. Just cut across the patterns at the knee. Spread the cut pieces apart as much as you want to add, and then tape a piece of paper in the gap. Reconnect the inseam and side cutting lines and you're done. Be sure to adjust both the front and back patterns by the same amount.

Let's make them

1. Sew 2 pocket pieces together with right sides facing, leaving a small opening in the top seam. Clip the corners, turn right side out, and press. Topstitch along the top edge of the pocket, closing the opening as you go (Figure 1). Repeat with the remaining pocket pieces so you have 2 finished patch pockets. Set aside.

2. Pin 1 finished pocket to 1 upper back leg. Repeat with the other pocket, taking care to ensure that the pockets are evenly placed on both legs. Stitch around the 3 sides of each pocket to create the back patch pockets.

3. Lay the 2 back pieces on a flat surface, right side up. Place the 2 front pieces on top of these, right side down. Sew each outside leg seam.

4. Fold 1 leg piece with right sides together and sew the inside leg seam. Repeat with the other leg.

5. Turn 1 leg inside out and place the other leg inside it, right sides facing and pockets matching; align the curved edges. Pin the curved crotch seam (Figure 2). Stitch this seam and then stitch again to reinforce. Turn the pants right side out.

6. Turn under a small hem (about ½″) along the top raw edge of the pants; press using a warm iron. Fold this under again to create a channel that is slightly wider (about 1½″) than the elastic. Press, pin, and topstitch in place, leaving a 2″ opening at the center back seam of the pants. You can also stitch along the top (just under the fold) of this channel if you wish.

7. Measure the elastic around the child's waist to obtain the correct length, or if this is not possible, 20″–22″ should be about right. Attach a chunky safety pin to the end of the elastic and thread it through the channel, taking care not to twist it. Overlap the elastic ends ½″ and sew them together securely. Stitch the opening in the channel.

8. Turn under the raw edge of a leg piece ½″ and press using a warm iron. Turn this edge under again, about 1″, and press again. Pin and then stitch the hem in place. Repeat this step with the other leg.

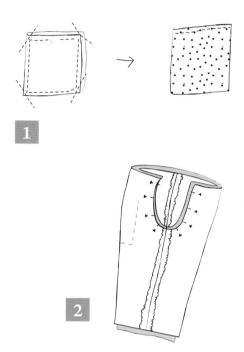

Kangaroo Pocket Sweatshirt

Sizes: 2T–4T

This is a simple and practical little garment

that your preschooler will enjoy wearing. Soft and comfortable knit fabric will keep him or her warm, and the big kangaroo pocket on the front is ideal for keeping treasures safe and on the body. From a maker's perspective, this simple design lends itself to customization—you can add anything you like to embellish the front pocket. Here I've hand appliquéd a little painted bird. In the past I've embroidered a paper plane on a pocket for my son. Have fun and use your imagination!

You will need

1½ yards of warm fabric*

¼ yard of cotton ribbing in a coordinating color

10″ × 13″ cotton fabric for the pocket lining

Fabric scrap or embroidery thread for embellishment

* You could use cotton knit sweatshirt fabric, fleece, or wool knit, or recycle an adult garment.

Cutting

Trace the pattern pieces (on tissue paper pattern sheet) for the front, back, sleeve, pocket, neckband, and cuff.

Sweater fabric

Cut 1 front piece (on the fold), 1 back piece (on the fold), 2 sleeve pieces, and 1 pocket piece.

Ribbing

Cut 1 neckband piece (on the fold) and 2 cuff pieces.

Cotton fabric

Cut 1 pocket piece for the pocket lining.

TIP
For longevity and interior neatness, it's a good idea to finish all the seams with a serger or by using the zigzag stitch on the sewing machine.

Let's make it

1. Sew the front and back pieces at the shoulder seams with right sides together.

2. Find the midpoint of each sleeve upper curve. Place a pin at that point. Match the pinned point with the outer edge of the shoulder seam. Pin the sleeve to the sweatshirt, with right sides together. Repeat with the remaining sleeve.

3. Sew the upper curved part of the sleeve to the sweatshirt armhole, easing to fit. Repeat with the other sleeve.

4. Make the kangaroo pocket by embellishing the pocket exterior piece (if desired), and then pin together the pocket exterior and pocket lining, right sides together.

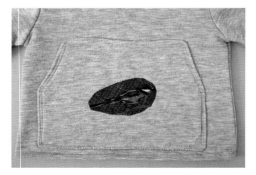

5. Sew all around the pocket pieces (this is much easier if you place the pocket lining on top when sewing on the machine), leaving a 4″ opening in the upper seam.

6. Clip the corners and trim the pocket seam allowances. Turn right side out through the opening. Tuck the seam allowance into the opening. Press flat.

7. Topstitch along each diagonal side of the pocket. Sew a second line of stitching about ¼″ from the first row on each diagonal.

8. Pin the finished pocket to the center front of the sweatshirt. Be sure to leave a couple of inches below the pocket to hem the sweatshirt.

9. Topstitch all around the pocket so that it is attached to the front of the sweatshirt, closing the opening. Leave the diagonal edges of the pocket unstitched, as these will provide pocket entry. Stitch again ¼″ inside the topstitching.

10. With right sides together, and beginning at the ends of the sleeves, sew each sleeve seam and side seam in one seam. Turn the sweatshirt right side out.

11. Stitch the short ends of the ribbed neck band together to make a tube. Fold the tube in half with wrong sides together so the raw edges meet. Repeat this step with each cuff.

12. Using the quartering method as described in the Snuggly Vest project (Step 3, page 71), sew the ribbed cuff pieces to the sleeve ends. Apply the neckband in the same way.

13. Fold the hem edge under ½″ and press. Fold under ½″ again, press, and pin in place. Stitch along the first fold.

Crossover Cardigan ------------------

Sizes: Can be made to fit any size

These wrap cardigans look so sweet on little girls, and they prove to be very warm and cute on small boys, too. To make these, I recycle two or more wool sweaters from a thrift shop, or perhaps some of my own that have seen better days.

You can finish the interior seams by serging or zigzagging them, but I find that after a few washes the seams fuse together naturally. Always wash the finished recycled garments in a cold machine wash and line dry them.

Pick two wool fabrics that are complementary, pair them up with some homemade bias tape, and you'll have a very unique garment.

You will need

1 cardigan or sweater that fits the child well to use as a pattern

2 or more large wool jersey sweaters, unfelted if possible (I find mine at thrift and secondhand clothing stores. Older styles tend to have better-quality fabric and higher wool content.)

Cotton bias tape, approximately ½″ × 112″ (See Making Bias Tape, right, to make your own.)

Making Bias Tape

1. Cut 2″-wide strips on a 45° angle to the grain of the fabric.

2. Piece strips together end to end to achieve the desired length.

3. Press the strip in half lengthwise with wrong sides together.

4. Open the strip and then fold the long raw edges ½″ (wrong sides together), so they meet in the middle.

5. Press in half again along the original fold.

Let's make it

Note: You will make your own pattern from an existing garment.

1. First, you need to make a pattern using the existing garment that
fits your child well. Alternately, you can just pin your child's garment
to the adult sweater and cut. Lay out the recyclable sweater and carefully cut it down the side seams so you are left with a large "back" piece
and a "front." Place the existing sweater along the bottom hem of the
big sweater and cut out a back piece that is roughly the same size as
the child's garment, taking care to ensure that the piece is symmetrical
(Figure 1). Set this aside.

2. You can cut the cardigan sleeves from the larger sweater. Line up
the "pattern sweater" on the bigger one, matching the cuff edges and
taking note of the sleeve width you are trying to achieve (see Figure 1,
page 105). Cut the sleeve shape you are after from the larger sweater.
You may need to resew the underarm seam of the new sleeve for a nar-
rower fit. Set the sleeves aside with the back piece (Figure 2).

3. Cut an angled front for the new cardigan. To do this, lay the freshly
cut back piece right side up and fold over the top right corner so that
you have a "pattern" for a sloped front. Carefully lay this shape onto
the remaining recycled fabric and cut it out, using the sweater's ribbed
band or hem.

4. From the second recyclable sweater, cut out another front to match, remembering that the front will slope the opposite way (Figure 3). Lay the cut cardigan pieces together and check that the shoulder seams and lengths are all roughly even. Trim as required. The leftover sleeves and back pieces can form the basis of the next crossover cardigan!

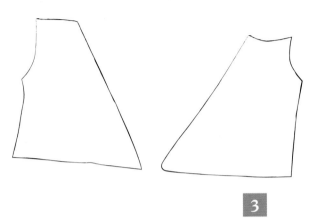

3

5. With right sides together, sew the 2 front pieces to the back piece at the shoulder seams. Sew the side seams, leaving a 2″ opening on one side seam for the tie to pass through (Figure 4).

6. Taking care to ensure that the right sides are together and the sleeve underarm seams are matched up with the cardigan side seams, pin and then sew the sleeves into the cardigan, easing to fit.

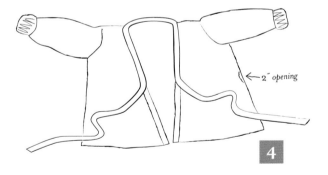

← 2″ *opening*

4

7. Position the bias tape along the angled edge of the cardigan front pieces, from the hem to about 8″ up the front. The exact measurement will depend on where the tie opening is located in the side seams so that the top of this bias piece is opposite the opening. Take care to stretch the binding, rather than the wool jersey fabric, as you go. Pin and stitch in place.

8. Find the center point of the remaining bias tape. Pin this to the center back neckline of the cardigan, and pin the rest of the tape along the neckline and sloping fronts of the cardigan, enclosing the raw ends of the front bias tape from Step 7 (Figure 4). Press the ties together and then stitch it all in place. Finish the ends of the bias tape by hand or machine; it's up to you. Thread one of the tie ends through the side seam opening and tie the cardigan closed in the back.

Snuggly Vest

Sizes: 2T–4T

This is a great little garment to make for a small one in your life. It's especially good for toddlers who are busy and active but need to stay warm. Simply throw on this wool vest and their arms will be free for making mud pies and exploring rock pools.

This simple pullover pattern works really well when recycling adult sweaters. Choose a warm cashmere or merino wool garment and use the original garment's ribbed hem to save time. You can even cut off the other ribbed parts of the sweater to use around the armholes and neckline if possible. Add a kangaroo pocket or appliquéd patch to make the vest one of a kind. For this vest, I used some thick wool jersey fabric I had on hand and added some bands of cotton ribbing. An appliquéd piece of cotton lawn fabric completed the look.

You will need

1 large adult pure wool sweater
or ½ yard wool jersey fabric

8″ of ribbing fabric (or use the ribbing bands on the recycled sweater)

Fabric scrap for appliqué (*optional*)

Cutting

Trace the pattern pieces (on tissue paper pattern sheet) for the vest front, vest back, neckband, armhole band, and hem band.

Wool jersey fabric or sweater

Cut 1 vest front piece on the fold and 1 vest back piece on the fold.

Ribbing

Cut 2 armhole band pieces.

Cut 1 neckband piece on the fold and 1 hem band piece on the fold.

Let's make it

1. With right sides facing, sew the vest front and back together at the shoulder and side seams.

2. Sew together the short ends of the bottom band to make a wide tube. Fold this piece lengthwise with wrong sides facing, so the raw edges are together.

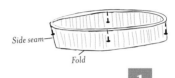

Side seam

Fold

1

3. Before sewing the piece from Step 2 to the bottom of the vest, you need to divide the hem band into 4 equal sections. To do this, place 4 pins around the folded band at equal distances. The seam of the band should be the starting point. Place a pin at the seam and another pin at the opposite side. Place a pin at each mid-point between the first 2 pins as well (Figure 1). Similarly, divide the vest bottom edge in 4 parts and mark with pins (Figure 2). Sew the hem band to the raw-edge hem of the vest, ensuring that the pins meet and the seamed part of the band is positioned at the back or side of the vest. You will need to stretch the ribbed band to fit the bottom edge of the vest, and this will draw in the finished vest at the hem a little.

2

4. Repeat Steps 2 and 3 to sew the ribbed bands to the armholes and neckline. Finish these seams by serging them or topstitching.

5. Hand appliqué the patch to the front.

Easy Wrap Dress

Sizes: 3T–4T (can be lengthened for a bigger size)

This is a simple little dress to make for your toddler. The beauty of it is in the wrap style, which can tie at either the back or front and is rather forgiving in form so that the dress will fit your girl for a long time. As she grows, it will become a short dress (or long top) to wear with leggings, and then you can pass it on to a little sister or friend. I've made this version in lightweight denim with contrasting handmade bias tape, but you could use lighter cotton for a summer dress or perhaps corduroy for a winter version.

You will need

1½ yards of cotton, denim, or corduroy nonstretch fabric

Approximately 5 yards of bias tape (See Making Bias Tape, page 64, to make your own.)

Cutting

Trace the pattern pieces (on tissue paper pattern sheet) for the dress back and front.

Cut 1 back piece on the fold.

Cut 2 front pieces (1 and 1 reversed) with the right sides of the fabric together.

Let's make it

1. Sew the dress back and 2 fronts, right sides together, at the shoulder seams.

2. With right sides together, sew the dress at one of the side seams.

3. Finish both edges of the unfinished side seam by serging or zigzagging. Sew together the seam, but leave a 2″ opening about 3″ from the armhole edge.

4. Apply bias tape to the unfinished lower front edges of the front pieces. Press and finish. Apply bias tape to the armhole edges (Figure 1). Press and finish.

5. Find the center point of the remaining length of bias tape and pin it to the center back neckline. Pin around the neckline and down the front angled edges. Stitch the bias tape in place (Figure 2). Press and sew the long ties on either side. Sew a narrow zigzag stitch along the raw edges of the tie ends to keep them from fraying.

6. Turn the hem under ½" and press. Turn under another ½", press, and stitch in place.

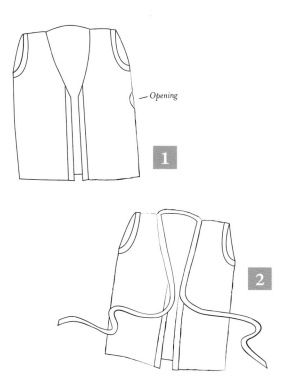

Dress-Up Cape

Sizes: Fits children
ages 4—10 and beyond

Almost all the children I know enjoy pretend play. My own son, being inherently rational, took quite some time to warm to it, but now he likes nothing more than wearing a silky cape over his ordinary clothes. And it's great to look out the window and see a garden full of kids reenacting a scene from ancient British royalty.

This cape is simple to make and is based on one in our dress-up box, originally made for my partner, Tom, when he was a pretend-play enthusiast himself. I have made these capes from many different fabrics: wool, silk, and velvet. Each has been received warmly by the little one in character. My son requested a green velveteen cape with ribbon ties, and I lined it with a royal blue cotton fabric. To make the cape for my daughter, I used an amazing old kimono that was too big for anyone I could think of. I used both the outer fabric and the robe lining, which was made of dip-dyed silk.

You will need

2 yards of fabric for the cape exterior
(I recommend nonstretch fabrics such
as velveteen, silk, cotton, or wool.)

2 yards of nonstretch fabric
for the cape lining

Approximately 50″ of bias tape or
1″-wide satin ribbon (See Making Bias
Tape, page 64 to make your own.)

Cutting

Trace the pattern piece (on tissue
paper pattern sheet) for the cape panel.

Outer cape fabric
Cut 4 cape panel pieces.

Lining fabric
Cut 4 cape panel pieces.

Let's make it

1. Sew together the outer panels down
each long edge, as shown in the diagram
(Figure 1). Press the seams open. Repeat
with the lining panels.

2. With right sides together, pin the finished
cape exterior to the cape lining along the side
seams and bottom, leaving an opening in
the bottom of about 4″. Pin together the top
edge and baste this seam with long stitches.
Stitch the side and bottom seams and turn
the cape right side out through the opening.

3. Press the cape well and hand stitch the
opening closed. Prepare the bias tape (or
press the wide ribbon so it is like bias tape).
Find the center point of the bias tape. Open
one side of the bias tape and pin it to the

center point of the cape top, leaving excess tape on either side of the cape. Stitch along the unfolded crease of the bias tape around the top of the cape. Trim away any seams or excess fabric at the top edge close to the bias tape stitching.

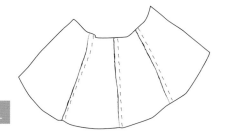

4. Press the bias tape closed over the neck stitching and, beginning at one end, machine sew together with a zigzag stitch to form ties on either side and to cover the top edge of the cape (Figure 2). Tie knots at the ends of the bias tape to prevent fraying.

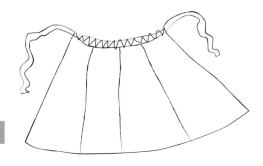

Art Smock

Sizes: 2T–4T

This is a handy little garment

to hang on a hook in your kitchen for
whenever artistic inspiration strikes. This
smock is simple to make, is loose fitting,
and ties at the back with bias tape, which is
also used to trim the neckline and pocket. It
features a pocket in which to store crackers
or crayons. It will easily fit over your
preschooler's clothes, protecting him or her
from paint, mud, or cake batter. Made up in
lightweight cotton, it would also make a sweet
beach top.

You will need

1¼ yards of cotton or linen fabric

1 package of bias tape (Or make
2 yards of your own from scrap fabric.
See Making Bias Tape, page 64.)

Cutting

Trace the pattern pieces (on tissue
paper pattern sheet) for the smock
front and back and pocket.

Cut 1 smock front piece on the fold.

Cut 2 smock back pieces.

Cut 1 pocket piece.

Let's make it

1. Sew together the smock front and smock
back pieces at the shoulder/arm seams, right
sides together. With right sides together, sew
together the underarm/side seams. Finish
these seams and press.

2. Make a small hem around the each sleeve
by folding the edges under ¼" twice. Press and
stitch in place.

3. Fold under ¼" on each side of the back
opening. Fold under ¼" again and press to
create a hem. Stitch in place (Figure 1).

4. Fold the lower edge under ¼" twice, press,
and stitch in place to hem the bottom edge of
the smock.

5. Trim the top edge of the pocket piece with
a length of bias tape. Serge or zigzag the sides
and bottom edge of the pocket piece. Using a

warm iron, press the pocket sides and bottom edge under ½". Center the pocket on the front of the art smock, pin, and sew in place along the sides and bottom. Determine the midpoint of the pocket and stitch down this line to create 2 smaller pockets (Figure 2).

6. Cut a 58" piece of bias tape. Fold out one side and press flat. Determine the midpoint of the tape and align it with the midpoint of the smock front neckline. Pin in place. Pin the bias tape all along the neckline, leaving the long edges on either side to form the smock ties. Using a narrow seam, sew the bias tape around the neck edge and trim the seam allowance.

7. Refold and press the tie edges. Beginning at one end, stitch along the ties, as close to the open edges as you can, until you reach the smock neckline. Keep stitching to secure the bias tape around the neckline, and continue until you reach the end of the other tie.

8. Trim all the threads and tie a knot at the end of each tie.

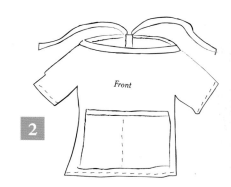

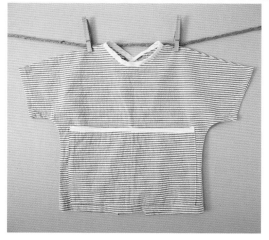

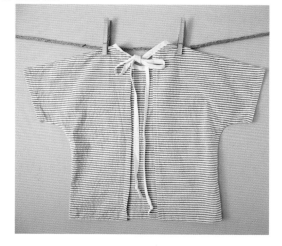

Foraging Satchel

Finished satchel: 11½″ × 11½″

I have been making these special little bags from natural linen since my daughter was about two and decided she needed a place to keep her natural treasures, of which, back then, she had many. We went on daily walks to explore our surroundings (we were living in the Norwegian countryside at the time), and she would come home with handfuls of acorns, wildflowers, feathers, and pinecones (or rather, *we* would come home with them). So *we* decided *she* needed her own easy-to-carry bag to wear on our outings.

This bag is made extra-special with a spot of hand embroidery on the front, but you could do some appliqué or add a pocket instead, if you prefer. I have provided some drawings that you could transfer to your linen with a soft pencil before embroidering, or you can come up with your own design.

You will need

¾ yard of linen fabric

½ yard of cotton fabric for the lining

7″ length of ribbon or cotton tape for the closure loop

1 button (A shank button works best.)

½ yard of 45″-wide fusible interfacing

Embroidery floss, needle, and hoop

Cutting

Trace the pattern piece (on tissue paper pattern sheet) for the bag.

Linen fabric
Cut 2 bag pieces

Cut 1 strip measuring 7″ × 24″ for the strap.

Lining fabric
Cut 2 bag pieces.

Interfacing
Cut 2 bag pieces.

Let's make it

1. Fold the bag strap piece in half lengthwise, with right sides together, and pin. Sew down along the raw edges. Turn right side out and then press with a warm iron so that the sewn seam runs down the center back of the strap. Fold in the raw ends, so that the edges are hidden, and press again (Figure 1). Set aside.

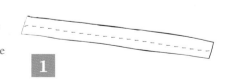

2. Find the center of one of the linen bag pieces and lightly sketch with a soft pencil the embroidery design. You can use a design you like by holding both the design and the linen up to a light or against a window and tracing the outline. Place the linen in the embroidery hoop and work the design. Embroidery stitches can be found on page 24 and a few motifs are shown on pages 25 and 89. Press the finished work.

3. Fuse the matching interfacing pieces to the wrong side of the bag exterior pieces. In addition to adding stiffness to the bag, it will keep the embroidery secure.

4. With right sides together, sew together the lining pieces along the bottom and sides. Turn and press. Repeat with the bag exterior pieces.

5. Bring the 2 ends of the 7″ ribbon or tape together so that it forms a loop. Find the center of the top edge of the back of the linen shell and pin the loop to the right side, so that the loop is pointing down and the ends are level with the raw edge (Figure 2). Turn the bag lining inside out. Place the linen bag (right side out) inside the lining bag. The right sides should be facing each other.

6. Pin around the top of the bag. Sew around the top, leaving a 4″ opening on one side and making sure you stitch over the loop ends.

7. Turn the bag right side out. Press the bag and pin the opening closed. Topstitch around the top edge of the bag, closing the opening as you go.

8. Pin the strap to the outside of the finished bag. Position the strap about 2½″ down the side of the bag and pin in place. Sew a square where the strap overlaps the bag, being careful to close the bottom of the strap where you pressed up the edges. Sew a neat "X" inside the square (Figure 3). Repeat on the other side of the bag.

9. Sew a button to the center of the front of the bag near the top edge, above the embroidery, so that the loop can be used as a closure.

It must be time to go for a walk to see what you can put inside the new foraging satchel.

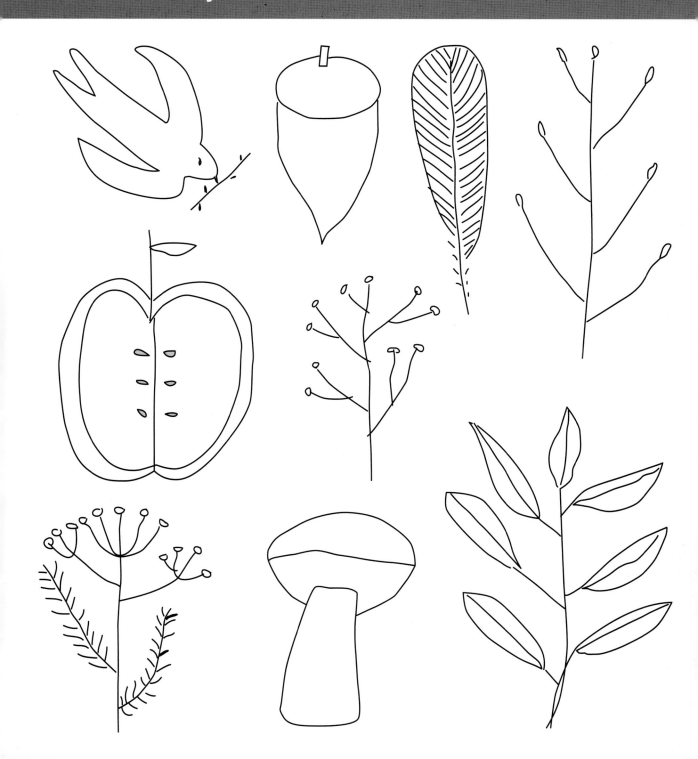

Everyday Skirt ----------------------------------

Sizes: Approximately 2T–5

This is a simple little skirt design, with a double-elasticized waistband for extra sweetness. The beauty of this simple "recipe" is that the skirt can be made up quickly and easily in any fabric you like. I have made this for "best" in beautiful pale embroidered linen or for winter school wear in fine corduroy. It also lends itself to embellishment; you could embroider something or add some lace or rickrack around the hemline. The stretchy waistband makes for a comfortable garment that any little girl will be happy to pull on herself.

You will need

1 yard of cotton fabric

40″–48″ length of ¼″-wide elastic
(See Cutting chart below.)

Large safety pin

Cutting

Mark out the skirt pieces with a yardstick and fabric pen or pencil. Try to cut the fabric on a selvage edge if you can, as this will save time later.	*Size (approximately)*		
	2T	4T/4	5
Cut 2 pieces of fabric measuring	15″ × 23″	16″ × 23″	17″ × 23″
Cut 2 pieces of elastic measuring	19″	21″	23″

Let's make it

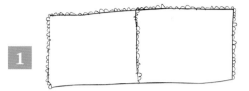

1. With right sides together, join the skirt pieces along one short side to create a large rectangle.

2. Serge or zigzag along the edges to finish the raw edges (if they are not selvages), leaving the hem edge unfinished (Figure 1).

3. Fold the top 2″ of each side under ¼″ to the wrong side and press this well, as shown (Figure 2). Topstitch along each 2″ folded side edge. Press.

4. With right sides together, sew the remaining side seam, beginning at the bottom and stopping where you stitched in Step 3 (Figure 3).

5. Press the top edge of the skirt under 2″. Carefully sew 3 parallel rows of stitching as follows to make "canals" for the elastic: Sew 1 row close to the folded edge, at the top. Sew another row of stitching close to the serged edge. Sew the last row in between these rows.

6. Hem the skirt by pressing under ½″ and then ½″ again to hide the raw edge. Stitch in place. Add a couple of rows of decorative stitching near the hem, if desired.

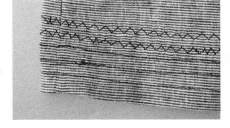

7. Use the safety pin to thread the elastic lengths through the channels at the top of the skirt. Overlap the ends and sew them together to secure. You can adjust these easily through the openings later if desired.

96

102

108

112

118

124

130

134

138

For Children

ages 5–10

Sunday Best Dress

Sizes: Approximately 4–6

Whether she's off to church,
lunch with family and friends, or the school
fair, every little girl needs a dress for "Sunday
best." Side pockets make this garment extra
useful and can contain such treasures as
skimming stones, sweets, or pocket money.

This dress could be made up in lightweight
cotton for summer picnics or fine corduroy
to be worn in winter with boots and tights. If
you're using a heavier fabric such as pinwale
cord, use lighter cotton fabric for the facings,
bias tape, and interior pockets. I was watching
the television series *Mad Men* while working on
this design, and I like to think there's a little of
the 1960s in it. There's just something about
the pleats that makes this dress a bit special.

You will need

2½ yards of nonstretch cotton fabric

Dressmaker's chalk or
a dissolving marker pen

1 package (or 1½ yards) of coordinating bias tape (See Making Bias
Tape, page 64, to make your own.)

Embroidery thread or ribbon
for the closure loop

1 small button

Cutting

Trace the pattern pieces (on tissue
paper pattern sheet) for the dress
upper front, dress back, pocket,
front facing, and back facing.

Cut 1 dress back piece on the fold,
4 pocket pieces, 1 front facing piece on
the fold, and 2 back facing pieces.

Cut 1 rectangle 27" × 45"
for the dress front.

Let's pleat and cut out the dress front

1. Fold the 27″ × 45″ rectangle in half so the folded piece measures 22½″ × 27″. Press a crease. Unfold the piece of fabric. On the right side, using a tape measure and dressmaker's chalk, mark 5 rows at 3″ intervals along the top on one side of the crease line. Repeat on the other side (Figure 1).

2. Pleat the fabric on one side of the crease line by bringing one marked line to another, ensuring that the pleat folds are facing away from the centerline. You should have 5 neat pleats pressed and facing away from the center. Repeat on the other side of the centerline, with the folds facing the opposite direction.

3. Press the pleats in place all the way down to the bottom of the fabric, using a nice hot iron. Use the longest stitch on the machine to baste the pleats in place from the top to about halfway down the fabric piece.

4. Fold the pleated fabric in half so that the right sides are facing each other. At the top of the piece, use the dress upper front template to cut the neckline and armholes of the dress front (Figure 2). Leave the pleat basting stitches in place at this point.

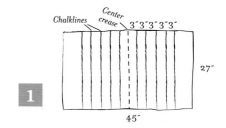

Chalklines Center crease 3″ 3″ 3″ 3″ 3″

27″

45″

1

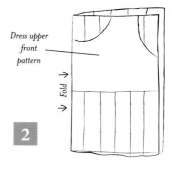

Dress upper front pattern

Fold

2

Let's sew the dress together

1. Sew together the dress front and dress back at the shoulder seams (Figure 3).

Sew together shoulder seams.

2. Sew the front facing and back facing pieces together at the shoulder seams. Finish (with pinking shears, zigzag stitch, or a serger) the bottom edge of the neckline facing.

3. Determine the center point of the dress back, press a crease, and then cut a 6″ slit down the back from the neckline edge.

4. With right sides together, pin the dress facing pieces to the dress neckline and then stitch in place. Trim close to the stitch line and press the seam. Fold the finished facing to the inside of the dress and press it in place (Figure 4).

5. Follow the markings on the dress back pattern to pin the pocket pieces to the side of the dress front, right sides together and with the pocket curve facing toward the hem of the dress (Figure 5). Repeat with the other pocket pieces on the dress back, ensuring that they are even with the front pocket pieces. Using a ¼″ seam, sew the pocket pieces to the dress where they are pinned; then press the finished seam toward the pocket.

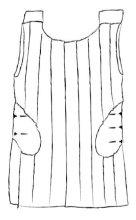

6. Pin the dress front to the dress back at the sides, remembering to pin around the pockets, too.

7. Stitch the dress side seams, using a ½″ seam. When you reach the pocket, pivot with the needle down, turning the work so that you include the pocket in the side seam (Figure 6). Repeat with the other side seam and pocket.

8. Use purchased bias tape or make your own from the dress fabric. Sew 1 side of the bias tape to the back slit, enclosing the dress back and facing. Press in place, and then hand stitch to finish. Hand stitch a thread or ribbon loop at the top edge of one side of the slit. Sew on a button to the top of the other side of the slit.

9. Apply bias tape to the armhole openings, press in place, and then hand stitch to finish.

10. Remove the basting stitches from the front pleats. Press under a narrow ¼″ hem at the bottom edge of the dress and then fold under another ½″. Press. Stitch the hem in place.

11. Carefully topstitch around the neckline, being sure that the facing and finished pleats are in place. Press the entire dress to finish.

6

New-Again Sweater

It can be tricky to find really warm wool cardigans and sweaters for children in the shops. Everything seems to be made from synthetic fabrics that easily pill and are designed for one season only. Using this method, you can make cardigans and sweaters for your children from old garments of your own or thrift store finds. With a little effort and time, you can recycle these into beautiful sweaters that will keep your little ones warm this winter.

You will need

1 sweater or cardigan that fits your
child well, to use as a pattern

1 large adult sweater or cardigan in good condition, washed and dried (I find that cashmere, merino,
and angora-blend wool fabrics are the best.)

1 package of premade bias tape or ½ yard of cotton fabric
(See Making Bias Tape, page 64, to make your own.)

4 buttons

Embroidery floss (*optional*)

Cutting

Use an existing garment that fits your child well as a pattern by laying it flat next to the garment to be recycled.

Note: First I will give instructions for making a cardigan, and then I will provide notes on making a sweater.

1. Cut out the sleeves by laying the pattern cardigan against the larger sleeves, matching the cuffs, and cutting a curved shoulder shape just above where the cardigan shoulder is (Figure 1). Use the freshly cut sleeve on the other arm as a template to ensure that the sleeves are both the same length. To narrow the sleeves, trim off the underarm seam and restitch. Set aside.

2. Cut the large garment into 2 pieces at the side seams and lay these pieces out flat.

Note: If you are starting with a large cardigan, you can line the front pieces up with the buttons and buttonholes already worked.

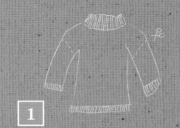

Fronts   Back

3. Lay the original cardigan on the back piece from Step 2 and cut out the back piece of the new garment. Use this piece as a template for cutting out the cardigan fronts; then cut the front piece in half lengthwise to create 2 front pieces (Figure 2). Arrange the new cardigan fronts on top of the back piece so that the wrong sides are facing each other. Check that the pieces are mostly even, and cut a gradual neckline curve in the back piece (keeping the left and right sides symmetrical) and a slightly more curved neckline in the front pieces (again, ensuring that the pieces are symmetrical).

Let's make it

Note: I use a serger to finish my interior seams and minimize fraying. If you don't have one, you could use a zigzag stitch or just leave the seams unfinished. If sewn securely, the seams should felt together fairly well after the finished garment has been washed and worn a few times.

1. Use a sharp machine needle and a long stitch to sew the cardigan's shoulder seams, with right sides together. Then sew the side seams from the armhole to the hem.

2. Pin each sleeve in place, right sides together, and stitch to the garment. You might need to stretch the cardigan body a little as you go to fit it.

3. Sew one side of the bias tape to the cardigan neckline. Try not to stretch the wool fabric too much; instead, stretch the bias tape as you go. Hand stitch to finish. Press.

4. Apply the bias tape to the cardigan front edges. Hand stitch to finish. If needed, sew the buttons, evenly spaced, onto one cardigan front edge. Work buttonholes on the other edge to match the buttons. I make these by hand with embroidery floss, but you could use a machine if you like. To do it by hand, whipstitch using floss along each side of a space big enough to accommodate the button. Then cut a slit between the two rows of whipstitches.

Variation:
Making a sweater

Follow the same guidelines on
page 106, but cut only one front piece
to match the back. If you want to use
bias tape for the neckline, cut a short
slit in the center back neck and apply
the tape around this slit; then sew a
button and loop closure to fasten.

If you wish to omit the bias tape alto-
gether, use some cotton ribbing to make
a stretchy neckband, or use any ribbed
part of the original garment. Pin evenly
around the neckline and sew in place.
Topstitch to finish.

Mix and Match Pants

Sizes: 4–6 years
6–8 years

This is a good, basic pattern for making pants for a child aged four through eight or so. The best thing about this design is that it can so easily be customized to the recipient and your climate! In winter these are cozy in soft corduroy, made up in the long length, with the lined patch pockets on the front for keeping small things safe. Or you could make back contrast pockets, as for Corduroy Pants to Grow In (page 54). In the warmer months, or for shorts-loving boys—like my own son, who will happily wear shorts all year round—you can make them into "long shorts." You decide!

You will need

2 yards of strong cotton fabric, such as denim, twill, or corduroy, for the pants

¼ yard of contrasting cotton fabric for the pocket lining

1 yard of 1″-wide elastic

Cutting

Trace the pattern pieces (on tissue paper pattern sheet) for the pants back, pants front, and pocket. (See Note, page 56, if you want to lengthen the pants.)

Pants fabric

Cut 2 pants back pieces, 2 pants front pieces, and 2 pocket pieces.*

Contrast fabric

Cut 2 pocket pieces.*

For pockets made from contrasting fabric, cut 4 pocket pieces from the contrasting fabric (2 for the pocket exteriors and 2 for the pocket linings).

Let's make them

1. Pin 1 pocket exterior piece and 1 pocket lining together with right sides facing (Figure 1).

2. Stitch all around the edge, leaving a 2″ opening in the center of the diagonal edge. Clip the corners and trim the seam.

3. Turn the pocket right side out and press. Topstitch along the diagonal edge, closing the opening as you go.

4. Repeat Steps 1–3 with the other pocket and set aside.

5. Lay the 2 leg back pieces on a flat surface, right side up. Place the 2 leg front pieces on top of these, right side down. Sew the outside leg seam on 1 leg. Turn right side out. Repeat with the remaining leg pieces.

6. Place the 2 leg pieces side by side, with the right side of each front piece facing up. Remembering that you will turn over the top edge of the pants for the elastic casing later, pin the pockets to each pant front, with the diagonal pocket edge toward the side seam of each leg piece.

7. Stitch around the pockets, remembering to leave the diagonal edge open (Figure 2). Press.

8. Turn the legs inside out and sew the inside leg seam of each piece.

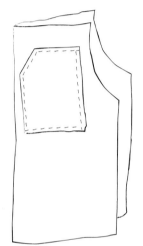

9. Place 1 leg inside the other, right sides facing, pockets matching, and curved edges matching. Pin the crotch seam (see Figure 2, page 57, for guidance). Stitch this seam and then stitch again to reinforce. Turn the pants right side out.

10. Turn under a small hem (about ½") along the top raw edge of the pants and press using a warm iron. Fold this under again to create a channel that is slightly wider than the elastic. Press, pin, and stitch in place, leaving a 2" opening at the center back to insert the elastic. You can also stitch along the top fold of this channel if you wish.

11. Measure the elastic around the child's waist to obtain the correct length, or if this is not possible, 25" to 27" should be about right. Attach a large safety pin to the end of the elastic and thread it through the channel, taking care not to twist it. Overlap the ends ½" and sew together securely. Sew the opening in the casing to close.

12. Turn under a ½" hem at the raw edge of the leg pieces, using a warm iron. Press. Turn this under again about 1" and press again. Pin and then stitch the hems in place.

Hooded Winter Coat

Sizes: 4–6 years
7–9 years

Every child needs a warm winter coat for the cold season—unless you happen to live on a tropical island. This is a simple coat pattern that works well for both boys and girls. I have made it a few times in vintage wool with a colorful cotton lining and also in a dark, thick corduroy for my son with matching-colored toggles to fasten. The front of the coat is slightly double-breasted for extra warmth, so I sew a chunky plastic snap inside to hold the front pieces together and to make it easy for children to do up themselves. Big vintage buttons or toggles make for a colorful and fun fastening on the outside of the coat.

You will need

2–2½ yards of thick fabric, such as wool or corduroy*

2–2½ yards of cotton non-stretch lining fabric*

1 large plastic snap

3 shank buttons or toggles

* Yardage depends on size of garment.

Cutting

Trace the pattern pieces (on tissue paper pattern sheet) for the coat front, coat back, sleeve, hood, and pocket.

Outer fabric

Cut 2 coat front pieces, 1 coat back piece (on the fold), 2 sleeve pieces, 2 hood pieces, and 2 pocket pieces.

Lining fabric

Cut 2 coat front pieces, 1 coat back piece (on the fold), 2 sleeve pieces, 2 hood pieces, and 2 pocket pieces.

Cut 2 strips 1″ × 7″ for closure loops.

Let's make it

1. With right sides together and starting with the armhole edge, match up the shoulder seams on the coat back and front pieces, and stitch (Figure 1).

2. Find the midpoint of the upper curve of the sleeve. Mark with a pin (Figure 2). Pin this point to the shoulder seam, right sides together, and sew this curved seam, easing to fit (Figure 3). Repeat with the other sleeve.

3. Sew the coat sides and sleeve, right sides together, in a continuous seam (Figure 4). Repeat with the other side and sleeve. Set aside.

4. Repeat Steps 1–3 to assemble the coat lining pieces. Set aside.

5. Sew the long curved seam of the hood exterior pieces, right sides together (Figure 5). Clip close to the seam and press. Repeat with the hood lining pieces.

6. Turn the hood lining right side out. Ensure that the hood exterior is still inside out. Place the hood lining inside the hood exterior so that the right sides are facing and the curves are matched. Pin the hood and lining together around the front curved edge (Figure 6) and stitch.

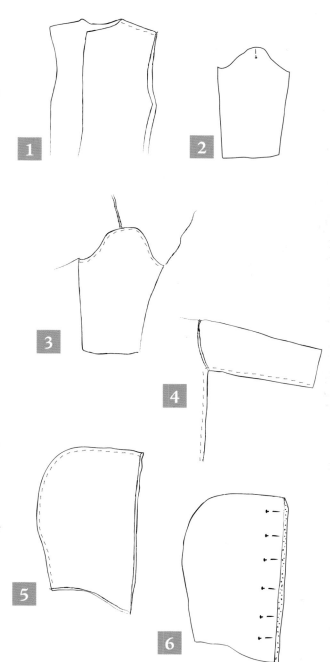

7. Turn the hood right side out and press. Baste the open edges together along the hood bottom (Figure 7).

8. Center the basted hood edge against the top edge of the coat exterior, ensuring that the hood exterior is facing the right side of the coat exterior. Pin and then baste in place ¼" from the raw, basted edge (Figure 8).

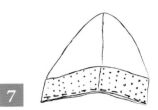

9. Stitch 1 pocket exterior and 1 pocket lining together, right sides together, leaving an opening along the top. Clip the corners and trim the seam allowances. Turn the pocket right side out and press. Stitch along the pocket top edge, closing up the opening as you go. Repeat with the other pocket piece and pocket lining.

10. Position the finished pocket on the coat front exterior, close to the side seam and about 3" above the bottom edge of the coat. Pin and then topstitch in place along the sides and bottom (Figure 9). Repeat with the other pocket on the opposite side of the coat front.

11. Fold a 1" × 7" closure loop strip in half lengthwise with right sides together. Stitch down the long raw edges. Trim the seam, turn right side out, and press. Repeat with the remaining closure loop strip. Set aside.

12. Ensure that the coat lining is inside out and the coat exterior is right side out. Pin the exterior and lining together along the top raw edge, right sides together. Keep the hood hanging down and sandwiched between the layers. Stitch along the neck edge using a ½" seam allowance.

13. Fold a closure strip from Step 11 in half and pin along the right front edge of the coat, 1½″ from the top. Fold the remaining strip in half and pin to the front edge, 2″ below the first loop (Figure 10). Now pin the coat exterior to the lining along the front edges and hem. Stitch the layers together, leaving a 6″ opening in the center of the hem.

14. Turn the finished coat right side out through the opening. Press and hand stitch the hem opening closed.

15. Take 1 sleeve and push the sleeve lining out of the way for a moment. Turn the raw edge under about ½″ and press. Now pull out the sleeve lining and press the raw edge under about ½″. Pin the pressed edges together and then stitch all around the sleeve edge. Repeat with the other sleeve.

16. Hand sew the snap to the top corner of the right coat front. Sew the corresponding snap piece in place on the lining of the left coat front (see photo below).

17. Position the buttons or toggles and sew in place.

Messenger Bag
with Pencil Case

Finished bag: 12˝ × 13˝

I first designed this bag for my son,

Arlo, who likes to ensure that his pens and pencils are with him at all times, accompanied by his latest Asterix book and paper for making some impromptu comic strips of his own. It's the perfect size for your child to carry, while taking responsibility for his or her own drink bottle, snacks, and pocket money on your next trip to town.

You will need

For the bag

¾ yard of strong cotton fabric, such as corduroy or denim

¾ yard of lining fabric (Lightweight cotton is best.)

½ yard of contrasting fabric for the flap (I've used sturdy linen/cotton canvas.)

½ yard of 45″-wide fusible interfacing

37″ length of wide cotton twill tape for the strap (average length for 8-year-old child)

10″ length of hook-and-loop tape

For the pencil case

Fabric scraps left over from the bag project

Fusible interfacing

8″ zipper

Cutting

For the bag

Bag exterior fabric:
Cut 2 pieces 12½″ × 14″.

Fusible interfacing:
Cut 2 pieces 12½″ × 14″ for the bag.
Cut 1 piece 10″ × 11″ for the flap.

Lining fabric:
Cut 2 pieces 12½″ × 14″ for the bag lining.
Cut 1 piece 10″ × 11″ for the flap lining.

Flap fabric:
Cut 1 piece 10″ × 11″.

For the pencil case

Bag exterior fabric:
Cut 2 pieces 4″ × 8″ for the case exterior from the bag scrap pieces.

Fusible interfacing:
Cut 2 pieces 4″ × 8″.

Lining fabric:
Cut 2 pieces 4″ × 8″ for the lining.

Let's make the bag

1. Apply fusible interfacing to the bag exterior and flap pieces.

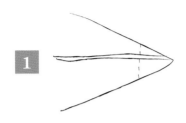

2. Sew along the sides and bottom of the bag exterior pieces, right sides together. To square the corners, pinch out the corners and sew across this seam 2″ from each corner (Figure 1). Repeat to construct the bag lining.

3. Align the outer flap and flap lining pieces and then round 2 corners of an 11″ side to create a curved bottom shape. Stitch together the flap exterior and lining pieces, with right sides together, using a ½″ seam allowance. Stitch the bottom, curved corners and side seams and leave the top seam unsewn. Clip the corner seams close to the stitching. Turn the flap right side out and press. Baste these pieces together, about ¼″ from the top raw edge (Figure 2).

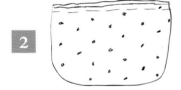

4. Pin the finished flap to one side of the bag top edge, so that the flap exterior is facing the bag exterior, right sides together. Baste this piece to the top of the bag exterior (Figure 3).

5. Pull the hook-and-loop tape strip apart. Center 1 part of the strip on the bottom of the flap lining; pin and stitch in place. Pin and stitch the other part onto the bag exterior, a couple of inches from the base (Figure 4). Make sure that it is pinned to the opposite side of the bag to which you have sewn the flap piece (see right photo, page 122).

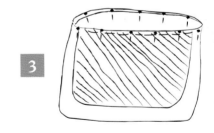

6. Ensure that the bag exterior is right side out. Turn the bag lining inside out. Place the bag exterior inside the lining so that the right sides are facing and the flap is hanging down on one side between the layers. Match the side seams and pin. Then sew with a ½″ seam all around the top, leaving a 6″ opening on one side. Ensure that you catch the bag, lining, and flap all neatly in this seam.

7. Turn the bag right side out through the opening. Press, pin, and then topstitch along the top of the bag, closing the opening as you go. I find this easiest to do with the bag exterior (rather than the lining) facing me.

8. Fold ½″ at the raw ends of the cotton twill tape and pin to the sides of the bag. Stitch in place by sewing a square with an "X" in the middle, as shown (Figure 5).

You can make the pencil case to match if you like.

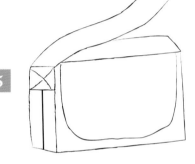

5

Let's make the pencil case

1. Apply interfacing to the 2 outer pieces. Sandwich the zipper between 1 exterior piece and 1 lining piece, with right sides together, so that the right side of the zipper is facing the exterior piece. Sew in place.

2. Flip these fabric pieces over and sandwich the remaining fabric pieces on either side of the opposite zipper edge in the same way. Sew down this seam.

3. Press the seams so that the zipper is in the middle and the lining and case exterior pieces are on either side. Topstitch along these seams, close to the zipper (Figure 6).

4. Open the zipper halfway. Place the case exterior pieces right sides together and the lining pieces right sides together. Stitch around 3 sides (Figure 7). Reinforce the stitching across either end of the zipper and clip the corners on the exterior pieces. Leave the bottom lining seam open.

5. Turn the case right side out again. Neatly fold and press the edges of the lining opening and stitch to close the opening. Push the lining inside the case and press to finish.

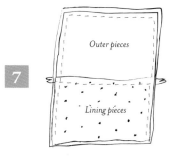

6

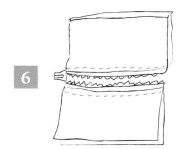

7

Outer pieces

Lining pieces

Velveteen Rabbit

Finished toy: 19˝ from top of head to toe

I was always a fan of the beautiful old children's book *The Velveteen Rabbit* by Margery Williams, but I must admit that these handmade rabbits of mine mostly came about from a deep love of cotton velveteen fabric. I found a thick blue velveteen curtain at a flea market, and it really wanted to be made into rabbits! I've made these in many colors, but my favorite remains a somewhat gothic black creature with a red silk ribbon that I made for my son.

I've noticed that children are instantly drawn to the lined rabbit ears. The ears are soft, silky, and generally pleasing.

Constructing the rabbit can be a little tricky and awkward toward the end, but I find the method gets easier with practice.

You will need

¾ yard of nonstretch cotton velveteen fabric

9″ × 12″ piece of cotton fabric
for the ear linings

Polyester fiberfill or wool stuffing

Embroidery thread and a small hoop

24″ length of ribbon

Cutting

Trace the pattern pieces (on
tissue paper pattern sheet) for
the body, leg, arm, and ear.

Velveteen

Cut 2 body pieces,* 4 leg pieces,
4 arm pieces, and 2 ear pieces.

Cotton fabric

Cut 2 ear pieces.

** It may be easier to transfer the body outline face
markings onto the velveteen and embroider the facing
using a hoop before cutting the body pieces.*

Let's make it

1. Use the pattern guidelines to trace the rabbit's face onto one of the body pieces. Use a soft pencil or tailor's chalk to transfer the features. Place this piece into the small embroidery hoop and embroider the rabbit's face. I use 2 strands of white floss for the eyes, nose, and mouth and 1 strand for the "stitch lines" above the face. Set aside.

2. Pin and sew together the rabbit's arms and legs, right sides facing, with small machine stitches, leaving the short straight end open. I like to reinforce these seams by stitching the seam a couple of times for strength. Clip close to the stitching. Turn the limbs right side out and stuff firmly. Remember to leave a small unstuffed space at the top of each limb, as this will make construction easier later. Set aside the finished arms and legs.

3. Place 1 velveteen and 1 cotton ear piece right sides together and stitch around the ear pieces in the same way that you made the arms and legs, leaving an opening at the base of the ear. Turn right side out and lightly press flat. Pinch together the top of the finished ear so that you fold over a small pleat in the raw edge (Figure 1). Baste across this pleat. Repeat this step to make the second ear.

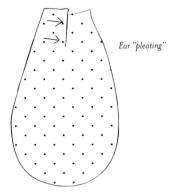

Ear "pleating"

1

4. Position the finished ears just outside the white "stitch lines" you embroidered on the rabbit face. The cotton side of the ear should be facing the right side of the rabbit front piece. Align the raw edges of the ears with the raw edge of the rabbit front piece. Baste in place close to the raw edge (Figure 2).

5. Lay the rabbit front piece right side up on a flat surface and, using the pattern markings for guidance, lay the stuffed rabbit arms in place, raw edges matching.

6. Lay the rabbit back piece over the front, right sides together, sandwiching the ears and arms between the 2 rabbit pieces. Pin the arms in place and pin all around the rabbit head, including the ears.

7. Sew the rabbit pieces together with a short stitch on your machine. Begin just below one of the pinned arms, stitch around the head, and finish just below the other arm. Turn the rabbit right side out and check that the arms are approximately symmetrical. If you are happy with the placement and stitching, you can turn the rabbit inside out again and reinforce the stitching. Press the seam with a warm iron.

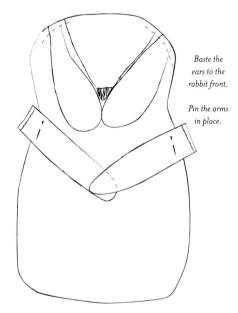

Baste the ears to the rabbit front.

Pin the arms in place.

2

8. With the rabbit inside out, take one of the stuffed legs and place it inside the rabbit body so that the raw edge is lined up with the raw edge of the rabbit body (see Linen Teddy, Figure 4, page 44, for guidance). Repeat this step with the other leg. Pin the legs in place and sew all around the rabbit body, leaving an opening on one side. This can be tricky, but be patient and check that you are catching all the edges together in the seam. Resew the seam at the bottom to ensure that the limbs are truly well attached.

9. Carefully turn the rabbit right side out through the opening you left. You will need to do this slowly, carefully pulling each limb out individually. If you are pleased with the limb placement, you can stuff the rabbit through the opening. Hand stitch the opening closed, using small stitches and strong thread.

10. Tie the ribbon around the rabbit's neck.

Pom-Pom Winter Hat

Sizes:
Hat fits a child approximately:
5—7 years (S), head circumference approximately 21˝
8—9 years (M), head circumference approximately 23˝

My children love to wear these simple hand-knitted hats, and I've been known to knit them for their friends, too. The garter stitch hat body provides cozy warmth, and the pom-pom adds a touch of old-fashioned fun. I've found this to be a good basic "recipe" for a child's hat, and if you have a young, budding knitter on your hands, you might like to pass the task of making one of these over to him or her. Children can at least help with the pom-pom, anyway.

You will need

Double-knit 8-ply worsted weight yarn (1 ball in the main color and 1 ball in the contrast color)

16" size 7 (4.5mm) circular needle

Set of double-pointed size 7 (4.5mm) needles

Darning needle

Small piece of lightweight cardboard, pen, and scissors for the pom-pom

Gauge

17 stitches and 34 rows in garter stitch = 4"

Let's make it

1. Using the circular needle and the contrast yarn, cast on 72 (size S) or 78 (size M) stitches and join, being careful not to twist the stitches. Place a marker at the join. Work in K2 P2 rib for 6 rows.

2. Change to the main color yarn and work in garter stitch (alternate rows knit and purl) until the work measures approximately 5" or 6" (depending on the size) from the cast-on edge. Finish with a purl round.

3. Place another marker at the end of this round, and then start decreasing thus:

+ *K9, K2tog, repeat from * to end of round.

+ Purl 1 round.

+ *K8, K2tog, repeat from * to end of round.

+ Purl 1 round.

4. Continue in this manner until knitting on the circular needle becomes difficult, then transfer the work to double-pointed needles. For the last decrease round:

+ *K3, K2tog, repeat from * to end of round.

+ K2tog to end. Cut the yarn, leaving a long end.

5. Use the darning needle to thread the long end of the yarn through the remaining stitches, remove them from the double-pointed needles, and draw up tightly to fasten together. Tie a knot and make a few stitches on the crown of the hat to secure the work.

Making the pom-pom

You can either leave the hat plain or embellish the crown with a pom-pom. Here is how I make a pom-pom:

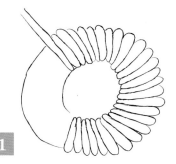

1. Trace around the top of a jar or mug so you have a circle measuring approximately 3″ in diameter. Cut 2 of these circles from the cardboard. Draw a smaller circle inside each circle (approximately 1½″ in diameter) and cut this shape out, so you are left with 2 donut-like pieces of cardboard.

2. Using a long length of contrast yarn, evenly wind the yarn around the 2 pieces of sandwiched cardboard through the hole (Figure 1) until the hole in the middle is almost completely closed with yarn.

3. Insert a scissor blade between the 2 layers of cardboard and snip the wound yarn around the edge of the pom-pom shape.

4. When you have snipped around the entire edge of the pom-pom, use a long piece of yarn to tie the middle of the work together, between the layers of cardboard. Save the tails of the long piece to attach the pom-pom to the hat (Step 5). Finally, remove the cardboard sandwich and "fluff out" the pom-pom. Trim any loose ends.

5. Securely sew the pom-pom to the top of the finished hat.

Pom-Pom Scarf

Finished scarf: Approximately 5½˝ × 32˝ (not including pom-poms)

This is a sweet and cozy scarf that could be made to match the pom-pom hat or a particular winter outfit. Much fun can be had in getting creative with color and texture here, and your kids can help you with the pom-pom making, too. The outer fabric of the scarf will provide good warmth and insulation, while the soft lining fabric will be a favorite against your child's skin. The pom-poms will add some weight and color to the whole garment, as well as looking very sweet on both boys and girls.

You will need

¼ yard of wool (or other close-weave and warm fabric)

¼ yard of soft cotton or jersey fabric

1 ball of yarn in a matching color

Cardboard scrap

Darning needle

Cutting

Outer fabric
Cut 1 strip 6″ × 33″.*

Lining fabric
Cut 1 strip 6″ × 33″.*

* You can cut 2 pieces 6″ × 16¾″ and sew them together end to end.

Let's make it

1. Place the outer and lining strips right sides together, pin, and then sew down both long edges of the scarf and across one of the short edges. If you are using a jersey fabric for the lining, take care not to stretch it as you sew, and ensure that the nonstretch fabric is on top as you work at the machine.

2. Finish the sewn edges with pinking shears or a zigzag stitch.

3. Turn the scarf right side out and press.

4. Turn under the raw edges at one end, press, and then stitch straight across to close the opening.

5. Make 2 pom-poms. Follow the instructions for pom-pom making in the Pom-Pom Winter Hat project (page 133). Use 5″ cardboard circles to make a large pom-pom.

6. Fold a large pleat across 1 short edge of the finished scarf so that you reduce the width of it to about 2½″. Stitch in place. Repeat with the other end.

7. Use a sharp darning needle and the end of yarn on the pom-pom to hand stitch a pom-pom to each end of the scarf as securely as possible.

Holdall Bags

Finished bag: Any size; example is 13" x 14"

These are useful bags or pouches
that can be made in nearly any fabric and any size
you can imagine. My children have pegs in their
bedroom to hang up bags of laundry, swimming
gear, library books, and Lego bricks or other toys.
You could make small pouches with oilcloth linings
for lunches or snacks or little bags from special
fabrics to keep treasures like marbles and jewelry safe
and organized. Just use your creativity.

The dimensions given prove useful for shoes or toys.

You will need

½ yard of fabric for the bag exterior

½ yard of fabric for the bag lining

¼ yard of fabric for the drawstring casing

2 yards of ribbon or cotton tape

Safety pin

Cutting

Exterior fabric
Cut 2 pieces 13″ × 14″.

Lining fabric
Cut 2 pieces 13″ × 14″.

Casing fabric
Cut 2 pieces 2″ × 15″.

Let's make it

1. Sew the bag exterior pieces together, right sides together, leaving the top 13″ edge unsewn. Repeat with the lining pieces, but leave a 3″ opening in the bottom seam (Figure 1).

2. Press under ¾″ on each short end of a casing strip. Fold each end under another ¾″ and press well. Stitch along the folds. Now fold the casing strip in half lengthwise, wrong sides together, and press (Figure 2). Repeat with the remaining casing strip.

3. Turn the bag exterior right side out. Center and pin 1 of the folded casing strips to the top edge of the right side of the bag exterior, aligning the raw edges. Pin in place and repeat with the other side of the bag exterior (Figure 3). Stitch the casings in place using a ¼″ seam allowance.

4. Make sure that the bag lining is still inside out. Place the bag exterior inside the lining so that the right sides are facing and the casings are sandwiched between the layers. Match the side seams and pin around the top. Stitch around the top, about ½″ from the edge, taking care to include all the layers.

5. Turn the bag right side out through the opening in the lining. Hand sew the opening closed. Push the lining into the pouch and press well so that the lining and exterior sit flat and the casings are standing up and away from the bag.

6. Cut the ribbon in half and attach a safety pin to an end. Thread a length of ribbon from a side seam through one casing, around the bag through the other casing, and out again where you started. Tie a knot to secure the ends. Attach the safety pin to the other piece of ribbon. Begin at the opposite side seam of the bag and thread it through each casing and back around to where you started. Tie a knot to secure the ends (Figure 4). Now, see what you can find to put in the new pouch!

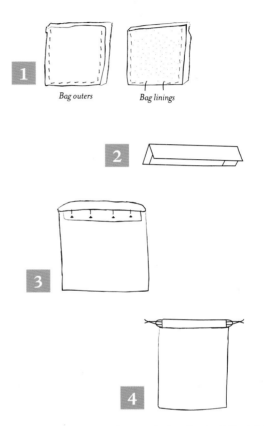

1

Bag outers   Bag linings

2

3

4

Chances are you'll want to make some of these projects to give as gifts. There's nothing like making something special to give to a new baby. You can direct all that love and expectation into a gift that will be treasured by the new parents, passed on to be used and enjoyed by future babies, and, if you make something like the slippers, quilt, or a velveteen rabbit, hopefully tucked away as a family heirloom later on.

If you've spent lots of time and creativity making your gift, why not wrap it beautifully as well? Gone are the days of store-bought gift wrap and plastic ribbons. If you think about it, you can use virtually anything to wrap your gifts.

As a keen secondhand-shop rummager, I like to collect interesting bits and pieces for future wrappings, and I keep everything together in a drawer, along with bits of ribbon, string, and the kitchen scissors. Use your imagination. You'll find you can happily recycle all sorts of papers and cards, saving them from the landfill and creating a most original and beautiful package!

Here are some wrapping ideas:

+ Brown paper and string is a classic and attractive way to wrap gifts. Use washi tape to secure the edges (washi tape is sticky paper tape from Japan, printed with interesting patterns and colors) and the parcel becomes even more stylish. You can also tuck a feather, a tiny bouquet, or branches under the string, or perhaps a wooden baby's rattle, along with your card.

- Be inspired by furoshiki, the Japanese tradition of wrapping gifts in a reusable cloth, such as a tea towel or tablecloth. Alternatively, you could find a vintage sheet at a secondhand store and wrap your gift in that. The book *Furoshiki Fabric Wraps* (C&T Publishing, 2012) by the Pixeladies (Deb Cashett and Kris Sazaki) offers some brilliant suggestions.

- Old maps, with their beautiful blues and greens, make gorgeous and interesting gift wrap. Team them with cardboard luggage tags to complete the faraway look.

- Your local charity shop might have a big box filled with particularly ugly old dressmaking patterns. You can save people from bad sewing experiences by buying these cheaply and using the tissue paper patterns to wrap delicate baby gifts. The newsprint instruction sheets look great as wrapping, too.

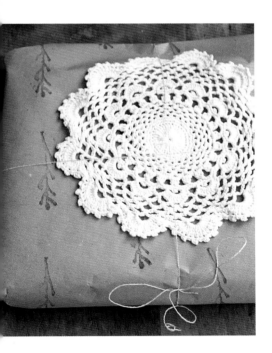

- You can download stylish designer gift wrap, offered free of charge on some websites. Alternatively, scan a favorite piece of vintage fabric and print it out for one-of-a-kind paper.

- Have fun carving rubber stamps from small erasers. Use these or purchased stamps to print your own wrapping paper. White ink on brown craft paper looks especially nice, as does colored ink on white paper. Small brown paper lunch bags can be stamped to present small gifts.

- Semisheer glassine bags can be easily sourced online. These look great with delicate baby gifts inside, fastened with colorful washi tape or a sticker.

- If you have a prolific preschool artist in your household, use his or her paintings as gift wrap. Or set up a workstation with a big piece of newsprint paper and colorful paints, and let the child make handprints all over for the most colorful and happiest gift wrap possible.

- The Holdall Bags project (page 138) in this book would make great reusable gift wrap. Make a bag in the appropriate size for your present, and tie a gift tag or card to the drawstrings.

About the Author

Melissa Wastney lives in Wellington, New Zealand, in an old wooden house near the city. She was raised on a farm in Nelson in a large family and has a deep love for creative work, children, and the natural world. She has two children, Arlo and Keira, with her partner, Tom.

Melissa has an arts degree from Victoria University, Wellington, and in the past has worked as a teacher, coffee maker, cook, and nanny. For the past five years she has kept a nearly daily blog, tinyhappy.typepad.com, to document her craft projects and inspiration and has enjoyed a wide readership from all around the world. She sells her textile work online and in various design stores and galleries internationally.